As one of the world's longest estab___ed
and best-known travel brands,
Thomas Cook are the experts in travel.

For more than 135 years our
guidebooks have unlocked the secrets
of destinations around the world,
sharing with travellers a wealth of
experience and ___sion for travel.

___ Cook as your
___our next trip
___ue heritage.

Thomas Cook **pocket** guides

# GLASGOW

Zoë Ross

Thomas
Cook

Your travelling companion since 1873

Written & updated by Zoë Ross

**Published by Thomas Cook Publishing**
A division of Thomas Cook Tour Operations Limited
Company registration No: 3772199 England
The Thomas Cook Business Park, 9 Coningsby Road
Peterborough PE3 8SB, United Kingdom
Email: books@thomascook.com, Tel: +44 (0)1733 416477
www.thomascookpublishing.com

**Produced by The Content Works Ltd**
Aston Court, Kingsmead Business Park, Frederick Place
High Wycombe, Bucks HP11 1LA
www.thecontentworks.com

Series design based on an original concept by Studio 183 Limited

ISBN: 978-1-84848-311-8

First edition © 2006 Thomas Cook Publishing
This third edition © 2010 Thomas Cook Publishing
Text © Thomas Cook Publishing
Maps © Thomas Cook Publishing/PCGraphics (UK) Limited
Reproduced by permission of Ordnance Survey on behalf of HMSO. © Crown
Copyright 2010. All rights reserved. Ordnance Survey Licence number 100035725.
Transport map © Communicarta Limited

Series Editor: Kelly Pipes
Production/DTP: Steven Collins

Printed and bound in Spain by GraphyCems

Cover photography (Stained glass rose, Charles Rennie Mackintosh) © Arcaid/Alamy

# CONTENTS

## INTRODUCING GLASGOW
Introduction..................................6
When to go...................................8
Magners Glasgow International
    Comedy Festival........................12
History ......................................14
Lifestyle....................................16
Culture......................................18

## MAKING THE MOST OF
## GLASGOW
Shopping.....................................22
Eating & drinking...........................24
Entertainment & nightlife .........28
Sport & relaxation.........................32
Accommodation ...........................34
The best of Glasgow.....................40
Suggested itineraries....................42
Something for nothing.................44
When it rains ..............................46
On arrival..................................48

## THE CITY OF GLASGOW
City Centre &
    Merchant City...........................60
The West End...............................78
Southside & River Clyde..............90

## OUT OF TOWN TRIPS
Clyde Valley................................106
Loch Lomond & the
    Trossachs National Park .......118
Stirling & Stirlingshire...............130

## PRACTICAL INFORMATION
Directory...................................144
Emergencies.................................154

## INDEX ..............................156

## MAPS
Glasgow ....................................50
Glasgow transport map..............55
City Centre &
    Merchant City...........................61
The West End ..............................79
Southside & River Clyde.............91
Clyde Valley ...............................107
Loch Lomond & the
    Trossachs National Park ........119
Stirling & Stirlingshire................131

## SYMBOLS KEY

The following symbols are used throughout this book:

ⓐ address ☏ telephone ⓦ website address ⓛ opening times
ⓝ public transport connections ❶ important

The following symbols are used on the maps:

| | | | |
|---|---|---|---|
| ⓘ | information office | ▦ | points of interest |
| ✈ | airport | ⊙ | city |
| ✚ | hospital | ○ | large town |
| 🛡 | police station | ○ | small town |
| 🚌 | bus station | ═ | motorway |
| 🚆 | railway station | — | main road |
| ⑤ | subway | | minor road |
| ✝ | cathedral | — | railway |
| ❶ | numbers denote featured cafés & restaurants | | |

Hotels and restaurants are graded by approximate price as follows:
£ budget price  ££ mid-range price  £££ expensive

The following abbreviations are used in the addresses:
Rd   Road
St   Street

◗ *The Glasgow School of Art was designed by Charles Rennie Mackintosh*

# INTRODUCING
Glasgow

# Introduction

Scotland's biggest city has a high opinion of itself – and with good reason. Glasgow has a vibrant arts scene, fostering cutting-edge musicians, painters and film-makers. Having given the world Lulu, more recently it has spawned bands such as Texas, Belle and Sebastian, Travis, Franz Ferdinand and The Fratellis. Its nightlife is legendary, with venues that host the biggest names in rock, pop, jazz and dance music. Scottish and Celtic traditional music is celebrated in many lively pubs and bars, and the city's restaurants offer a menu that extends from the best of modern Scottish seafood and game to superb Indian, Thai, Chinese, Japanese, Tex-Mex and Asian-Pacific fusion dishes.

Glasgow has high culture too. The city is home to Scottish Opera, Scottish Royal Ballet, the BBC Scottish Symphony Orchestra, the Glasgow School of Art, and some of Britain's finest museums and art galleries. It can – and does – claim to be Scotland's sporting capital, with a keenly contested rivalry between the country's two top football teams, Rangers and Celtic, as well as its international stadium at Hampden. The city will host the Commonwealth Games in 2014, which will put its sporting facilities on the world stage. In addition, Glasgow is Scotland's media hub, and since the 1980s has been a centre for cutting-edge design and top-end shopping.

While it is an intensely urban place – the heart of a conurbation that sprawls across more than 650 sq km (400 sq miles) of southwest Scotland and is home to almost half the country's population – Glasgow has plenty of green spaces, with landscaped parks and city gardens laid out during the 19th century. The River Clyde winds through the heart of Glasgow on its way to the Firth of Clyde and the Atlantic, and the Scottish highlands and islands are surprisingly close to the city centre. Islands such as Bute and Arran are less than an hour away, and the wide open spaces of Loch Lomond and the Trossachs are within easy reach.

And although the psychological gulf between the stereotypically bold, brash Glasgow and well-bred, genteel Edinburgh sometimes seems unbridgeable, Edinburgh is in fact fewer than 40 minutes away by rail, so its attractions are also easily accessible, even on a short break.

▲ *George Square is dominated by the grand City Chambers*

# When to go

A visit to Glasgow will reward you at any time. The city has plenty of indoor attractions for a winter trip – not all of them pubs – but it is undeniably more attractive in spring (April to May), when early blooming daffodils, tulips and crocuses bring a blaze of colour to its parks and gardens. In summer, long, light evenings allow plenty of time for exploring. September and October, as leaves turn autumnal and early frosts bring crisp, clear days, can be perfect times for trips out of town.

## SEASONS & CLIMATE

Scottish weather is noticeably colder than southern England's, but Glasgow's climate is mellowed by the Atlantic. Temperatures rarely fall to freezing point, even in mid-winter, and only rarely rise as high as 25°C (77°F) in mid-summer. However, that same Atlantic influence means that overcast skies and rain are not unlikely at any time of year, so come prepared. If you plan to venture beyond the city into the hills and moors of Argyll or to walk a stretch of the West Highland Way, good boots and waterproof clothing are essential.

## ANNUAL EVENTS

### January

**Hogmanay** New Year's Eve is raucously celebrated all over Scotland, and Glasgow's Hogmanay is no exception. It kicks off in George Square at 21.00 on 31 December and carries on until well into the early hours, featuring live rock, traditional music and family entertainment. Tickets cost around £15. ❶ (0141) 302 2845

**Celtic Connections** A three-week festival in which big names of the Celtic tradition from as far away as Canada, the USA and

Australia descend on the city with their fiddles and pipes.
ⓦ www.celticconnections.com
**Burns Night** (25 Jan) The birthday of Scotland's national poet is celebrated with whisky, haggis, pipe music and poetry.

### February
**Glasgow Film Festival** A showcase for work by leading Scottish and international film directors. ⓦ www.glasgowfilmfestival.org.uk

### March
**St Patrick's Day** (17 Mar) Given the Irish roots of so many Glaswegians, it's not surprising that St Patrick's Day is a popular celebration in many pubs.

↻ *Christmas lights in Glasgow's Exchange Square*

**Magners Glasgow International Comedy Festival** A cackle-fest of charismatic kings and queens of comedy (see page 12).

### April
**Glasgow International Festival of Contemporary Visual Art**
Adventurous and challenging commissioned work and installations are showcased. Ⓦ www.glasgowinternational.org

### June & July
**Glasgow West End Festival** (second two weeks June) In which Glasgow pretends to be Rio, with fabulous carnivals, the Midsummer Carnival parade and much whooping it up. Ⓦ www.westendfestival.co.uk

◆ *The West End Festival parade is a joyful and entertaining celebration*

**Glasgow International Jazz Festival** (end of June) Venues across the city get rhythmic for a festival that's attracting bigger and bigger names. As well as the main events, look out for free 'fringe' jazz performances in the city's bars and cafés. Ⓦ www.jazzfest.co.uk

**Bard in the Botanics Summer Shakespeare Festival** A month of open-air drama spanning June and July to celebrate Shakespeare. Ⓦ www.bardinthebotanics.org

**Merchant City Festival** (end of July or September) A feast

of music, drama and visual arts. And fashion. And food.
Ⓦ www.merchantcityfestival.com

**August**
**Glasgow International Piping Festival** (second week Aug) No, not cake decorating – bag-piping, along with many other manifestations of tartan culture in this city-wide fest. Ⓦ www.pipingfestival.co.uk

**September–November**
**Whisky Live** Part of a European-wide whisky-tasting event. Eat, drink, drink some more and debate the merits of the single currency. The fun takes place in September; check listings for exact dates.
Ⓐ George Square Ⓦ www.whiskylive.com
**Glasgay!** Britain's largest gay arts festival, with film, theatre, comedy and music. Events run from September right through to the beginning of November. Ⓦ www.glasgay.co.uk

---

**PUBLIC HOLIDAYS**
**New Year Bank Holidays** 1 & 2 Jan
**Good Friday** 22 Apr 2011, 8 Apr 2012, 31 Mar 2013
**May Bank Holiday** 1st Mon in May
**August Bank Holiday** 1st Mon in Aug
**Christmas Day** 25 Dec
**Boxing Day** 26 Dec

---

Public holidays are similar to those in England but do not include Easter Monday. Instead, Scots take two days off to recover from Hogmanay (see page 8).

# Magners Glasgow International Comedy Festival

Glasgow is steeped in comedy. No matter which pub or bar you happen to walk into, you'll meet at least ten people who are miles funnier than anyone you'll ever see on TV. And, on a more formal level, two of the Godfathers of the UK stand-up scene, Billy Connolly and Jerry Sadowitz, both grew up and rose to prominence in the city.

It's appropriate, then, that Glasgow plays host to one of Britian's most popular and influential comedy festivals: every March, for just over two weeks, the city stages the **Magners Glasgow International Comedy Festival** (Ⓦ www.glasgowcomedyfestival.com). Growing in scope and popularity every year since its inauguration in 2002, it has proved a sure-fire hit, bringing some much-needed light heartedness at the end of every winter and – no less important – proving that Edinburgh isn't the only city in Scotland that has a high-profile chuckle-fest.

Venues all over the city are utilised for the event, from the smallest pub theatre to the renowned Stand Comedy Club (see page 30), to large-scale auditoriums such as the Theatre Royal (see page 18). Even going out for a quiet drink is likely to prove difficult, as many of the city-centre bars get in on the act. Actually, even going out for a quiet walk in the town centre can be tricky while the festival is on as gigs often spill out into the streets and become decidedly free-form (which might be a euphemism for rowdy).

The reputation of the festival has grown in a remarkably short space of time, so much so that big-name British comedians such as Russell Brand, Paul Merton, Ronnie Corbett and Jimmy Carr are keen to sign up to the programme. International names such as Joan Rivers also descend on the city to enlighten audiences (which number around 40,000 people) with their own brand of humour.

There are over 350 shows staged in more than 50 venues over the fortnight. And it's not all lager-fuelled stand-up: some events are geared exclusively towards children, while comedy drama is staged at venues such as the Citizens Theatre (see page 18). Additionally, there are some improvisational comedy events and comic films (at Glasgow Film Theatre, see page 28), which all form part of this laugh-along.

Tickets sell out fast, particularly for the big-name shows, but can be obtained online or by phoning ☎ 0844 395 4005.

○ *A great night out at The Stand Comedy Club*

# History

The site where Glasgow city centre now stands was settled as early as AD 550 by monks from Ireland, led by St Mungo. Glasgow's first cathedral, named after St Mungo, was consecrated in the 12th century AD. The city's university was founded in 1451.

Handily located between the Highland and Lowland regions, Glasgow became a prosperous medieval trade centre and port – and it was less vulnerable than Edinburgh, the country's capital, to English invasion.

But it was the union of Scotland with England in 1707 that made the city its first fortune, allowing it to import tobacco, sugar and rum from English colonies in America and the Caribbean that had been closed to Scottish trade until then. Some of the most impressive buildings of Glasgow's Merchant City district date from these 18th-century boom years.

The Atlantic trade was damaged by the secession of Britain's American colonies in 1776, but Glasgow's entrepreneurs branched out into other industries. The city was perfectly placed to take advantage of the new technologies of the Industrial Revolution, with coalfields and iron ore on its doorstep and the River Clyde as its gateway to world markets. In the 19th century it became one of the powerhouses of British industry and the greatest ship building city in the world – the words 'Clyde built' became synonymous with sturdy reliability.

Glasgow also had two handy sources of labour close by. In the 1840s the Scottish Highlands and Ireland were struck by famine, and hundreds of thousands of people were drawn to the city in search of work. Glasgow's urban slums became a byword for social deprivation, while its industrial workers became a vanguard of the labour movement. Meanwhile, many wealthy capitalists endowed the city with grandiose public buildings, museums and concert halls, and the city became a noted centre for the arts and sciences.

World War I, the decline of the British Empire and the depression of the 1930s all hit Glasgow hard, and German air raids on the shipyards of the Clyde caused much damage and loss of life during World War II. Post-war Glasgow sank into decline as the heavy industries on which its economy was based collapsed, and the search for new sources of employment and prosperity seemed fruitless. Well-meant efforts to re-house the city's workers in the 1950s and 1960s often backfired, with new housing estates such as Easterhouse displaying many of the same intractable social problems as the city's slums. Drug and alcohol abuse and violent crime remain an issue in Glasgow's deprived suburbs even today.

With the 1980s, however, came an upturn in Glasgow's fortunes as service industries made an impact on unemployment, and the city began to reinvent itself as a cultural capital and centre of educational excellence. In the early years of the 21st century, Glasgow has rebuilt its reputation as one of Europe's most vibrant and youthful cities. With the 2014 Commonwealth Games to look forward to, the city is ready to take its rightful place on the world stage.

◆ *Glasgow's cathedral dates from the 12th century*

# Lifestyle

Glasgow prides itself on its friendliness – and Glaswegians love to draw mischievous comparisons with Edinburgh and the capital's reputation for dour reserve. It's certainly easier to fall into conversation with Glaswegians than with the natives of virtually any other British city. Football is of course a favourite topic, and any male expressing a lack of interest in the beautiful game will be regarded with sympathetic disbelief. But before expressing support for one or other of Glasgow's 'Old Firm' teams, be aware that football loyalties are deep and passions run high.

The traditional Glasgow lifestyle, with its high consumption of alcohol, tobacco, fried food, sugar and salt, is notoriously the least healthy in Europe. In some of the city's poorest areas, male life expectancy is under 60 years, with heart disease and cancer the main killers. But a wider choice of diet and campaigns against alcohol abuse and smoking are gradually easing young Glaswegians towards a healthier lifestyle than that of their parents – not least because many younger people recognise that smoking and sporting fitness are incompatible.

Glaswegians love dressing up and going out – especially at weekends. That said, bars, clubs and pubs are lively almost any night of the week. These days, classy bars almost outnumber old-style pubs in the city centre. Glaswegians are also among the world's most enthusiastic film-goers.

Sport – which in Glasgow mostly means football – is an obsession. For most Glaswegian males Saturday afternoon is sacrosanct to the game, and it's virtually impossible to find a bar or pub without a TV screen tuned to the day's big fixture.

With a climate that can turn cold and wet at any time, Glasgow's lifestyle is an indoor one for much of the year. Ironically, the ban o 1 smoking in public spaces has created an instant outdoor drinking culture, with many pubs and bars offering outdoor tables – sheltered by umbrellas and warmed by gas heaters – to evade the ban.

There's also a long and healthier tradition of getting out of the city on summer weekends to take a ferry 'doon the watter' to the islands of the Firth of Clyde, spend a day on the beaches of Ayrshire, walk in the hills of Argyll or the Pentlands, or sail on Loch Lomond (see page 123).

◆ *Enjoying an outdoor drink at a street café*

## Culture

Glasgow emerged from the cultural shadow of Edinburgh in 1990, when against the odds it won the European City of Culture title, ushering in an exciting new era for the arts. But in truth the city already had a strong cultural background that spanned high art – in the shape of ballet, opera, classical music, painting and sculpture – as well as the glorious humour of music halls and comedy theatres. Both still flourish.

Edinburgh may be the Scottish capital, but it is Glasgow that is home to most of the national performing companies. In terms of classical music, the BBC Scottish Symphony Orchestra and Scottish Opera (which performs classics in its annual Opera in the City concerts) are both based here.

Glasgow also takes the lead on matters theatrical. The **Theatre Royal** (ⓐ 282 Hope St ⓣ (0141) 240 1133 ⓦ www.ambassadortickets.com/glasgow) and the **King's Theatre** (ⓐ 297 Bath St ⓣ (0141) 240 1111 ⓦ www.ambassadortickets.com/glasgow) both stage touring West End productions, usually large-scale musicals. The **Tron** (ⓐ 63 Trongate ⓣ (0141) 552 4267 ⓦ www.tron.co.uk) is home to more avant-garde productions, as well as contemporary dance, jazz concerts and comedy acts. The **Citizens Theatre** (ⓐ 119 Gorbals St ⓣ (0141) 429 0022 ⓦ www.citz.co.uk) is the city's repertory theatre, staging new works by both Scottish and international playwrights.

The popular **National Theatre of Scotland** (ⓐ 25 Soutra Place, Cranhill ⓣ (0141) 221 0970 ⓦ www.nationaltheatrescotland.com) puts on experimental performances all around the country as well as in various different venues in Glasgow.

---

▶ *The BBC Scottish Symphony Orchestra*

The **Scottish Ballet** (ⓐ 261 West Princes St ① (0141) 331 2931 Ⓦ www.scottishballet.co.uk) has had a great resurgence of late, performing newly commissioned pieces.

Many of Glasgow's 19th-century plutocrats became patrons of the arts, endowing the city with world-class art galleries and museums such as Kelvingrove Art Gallery & Museum (see page 82) and the amazingly eclectic Burrell Collection (see page 97).

The most famous artist and designer associated with Glasgow is, of course, Charles Rennie Mackintosh. In order to fully appreciate his great vision you can buy a one-day ticket that covers the 'Mackintosh Trail', taking in sights such as the Scotland Street School Museum (see page 101). For more information, check Ⓦ www.crmsociety.com. You can obtain Mackintosh Trail Tickets online or from tourist information centres (see page 152).

The Glasgow School of Art (see page 68) also designed by Charles Rennie Mackintosh in 1896, has fostered a huge number of talented artists. Work by cutting-edge daubers is on show at the annual Glasgow International Festival of Contemporary Art (see page 10), held each year in April on George Square and at the prestigious Glasgow International Exhibition in May.

Glasgow was born out of the Industrial Revolution and many of its museums are keen to preserve this history, including the Clydebuilt Scottish Maritime Museum (see page 98), which examines how important the river was to the success of the city. Glaswegians' roots are also very much in sport, and to really understand the culture of the city's residents you should visit at least one of the three football museums: the Scottish Football Museum (see page 100), Celtic FC Visitor Centre (see page 90) or Rangers Football Club (see page 93).

---

▶ *Twenty-first century Glasgow*

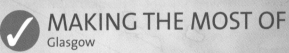

# MAKING THE MOST OF
### Glasgow

# Shopping

If you're a shopaholic you'll love Glasgow, particularly if you're after designer names and high-end high-street gear. There's a fair share of typical Scottish goods such as tartan, cashmere or whisky, but Glasgow is far more focused on style than souvenirs.

The main shopping area in the city centre is the pedestrianised triangle that is Sauchiehall Street, Argyle Street and, most importantly, Buchanan Street. Here you'll find many indoor shopping areas as well as high-street fashion outlets like Karen Millen and Hobbs, and department stores.

The Merchant City area and the West End, particularly Byres Road, are the primary central areas for second-hand goods such as clothes and books as well as antiques at places such as **De Courcy's Antique Craft Arcade** (ⓐ 5 Cresswell Lane (off Cresswell St) ⓣ (0141) 334 6673). Antiques are also a major feature at the Scottish Exhibition and Conference Centre (see page 94).

Glasgow abounds with indoor shopping areas – no bad thing given the high chance of rain at any given time of day or year. The best-known and most elegant shopping centre in the city is Princes Square (see page 72) on Buchanan Street, where quality brand-name shops sell their wares over a four-floor emporium with stylish cafés on the basement level.

Buchanan Galleries (see page 70) is less sumptuous but larger. The 19th-century **Argyll Arcade** (ⓐ 56 Argyll Arcade ⓣ (0141) 221 3781 ⓦ www.argyll-arcade.com) is reminiscent of London's elegant Victorian arcades and is lined with more than 30 jewellers. The vast St Enoch Shopping Centre (see page 72) is more family orientated and concentrates on high-street chains. Meanwhile, **Victorian Village** (ⓐ 39 West Regent St ⓣ (0141) 332 0808) has its focus strongly in the past, and is a great place for vintage clothing and costume jewellery.

Merchant Square in Merchant City (see page 71) is the ideal place for gifts, while the Italian Centre (see page 70) brings the best of Italian design in both household goods and clothing to Glasgow.

One of the most famous markets in the country is The Barras, an antique-cum-flea market just to the east of the city centre (see page 70). If it's a nice day, prepare to spend at least a couple of hours here browsing the stalls and jostling with locals and the vociferous market traders.

◯ *Buchanan Street is a major shopping area*

# Eating & drinking

Scotland may still have a reputation for serving everything fried, but in recent years Glasgow has earned the tag as one of the best places to eat in Britain outside London. There is a vast array of top-class restaurants, fashionable cafés and bars all over the city, as well as a wide range of budget options. Pub culture is, of course, alive and well, and there are plenty of traditional meals to be had. Unlike Edinburgh, though, Glasgow has embraced modernity with vigour, and if you're after trendy décor while you drink, this is the city for you.

Scottish restaurants focus heavily on meat and fish, although vegetarians should be able to find a suitable option. **Mono** (③ 12 King's Court, off King St ❶ (0141) 553 2400 ❷ 12.00–00.00 Sun–Thur, 12.00–01.00 Fri & Sat) is a great vegetarian restaurant with occasional live music.

There's no hard or fast rule as to whether restaurants include service charges on their bill or not – some do and some don't. So check your bill when paying. If service is not included, it's customary to leave a tip of 10–15 per cent of the cost of the meal. Tips aren't required in pubs if you're only drinking, even though some bars have the annoying habit of returning your change in a saucer in

## PRICE CATEGORIES

The following price guide, used throughout the book, indicates the average price per head for a two or three course à la carte dinner, excluding drinks. Lunch will usually be a little cheaper in each category and many restaurants also offer fixed-price menus.

£ up to £25   ££ £25–35   £££ over £35

🔺 *Café culture, weather permitting, Glasgow style*

the expectation of a little gratuity.

Lunch is usually served between 12.00 and 14.30, and dinner between 18.00 and 23.30, but many restaurants stay open all day with a continuous service.

All public places in Scotland, including restaurants, pubs and bars, are strictly non-smoking.

Glasgow has the best reputation for Indian food in Scotland, so if you're a curry fan you'll be spoilt for choice here. Asian restaurants can be found all over the city, but particularly in the West End district.

Italians began to emigrate to Glasgow in the 1850s and the first half of the 20th century, and today the city has the third-largest Italian community in Britain. Many of the immigrants turned to catering to earn their living, and Glasgow boasts a long tradition of Italian food, from elegant restaurants and family-run trattorias to Italian delis and cafes. These two national cuisines may dominate, but all manner of ethnic food can be found in the city, from Greek to Mexican to Thai to Japanese.

Meat plays an important part in Scottish cuisine and you'll see plenty of Aberdeen Angus beef, venison and lamb on restaurant menus, and game such as pheasant and partridge in season. Cullen Skink is a delicious haddock and potato soup that is very heartening on a cold winter's day, while Arbroath Smokies are smoked haddock that originate from the eastern coastal town of Arbroath. And, of course, fish and chips (known as a 'fish supper' in Scotland) of high quality are available all over the city.

For a savoury snack many bakers sell Bridies, which are a take on the Cornish pasty but made with puff pastry instead of shortcrust. Another savoury snack is the oatcake, delicious when served with Scottish cheeses. For a sweet teatime snack you can't go wrong with traditional Scottish shortbread. Ice cream, too, has a long-standing

## HAGGIS

Haggis is probably the most famous Scottish dish, although its description may not appeal to all tastes. Similar to a ball-shaped sausage, it consists of sheep's intestines, heart and liver, minced with onion, oatmeal and various spices. The mixture is stuffed into the animal's stomach lining, then boiled and traditionally served with mashed swede and potato ('neeps' and 'tatties'). If the real thing doesn't appeal, vegetarian haggis made with pulses, vegetables and nuts is increasingly available, although most Scots find the notion an aberration.

tradition in Glasgow, given its large Italian community.

Whisky, both malt and blended, is the most famous Scottish drink. Much of it is made in distilleries around the country, but Glasgow also boasts two distilleries of its own. Tours of **Whyte & Mackay** (🇦 310 St Vincent St 🇹 (0141) 248 5771 🇼 www.whyteandmackay.co.uk) and the **Speyside Distillery** (🇦 Duchess Rd, Rutherglen 🇹 (0141) 647 4464 🇼 www.speysidedistillery.co.uk) can be arranged. Glasgow also has its own brewery, **Tennents Caledonian** (🇦 161 Duke St 🇹 (0141) 552 6552), right in the centre of the city, which brews the famous Tennents lager.

The Glasgow Farmers' Market is the city's best food market, selling fruit, vegetables, game, seafood and Scottish cheeses. The market is held at Queens Park on the Southside of the city on the first and third Saturday of each month and at **Mansfield Park** (🇦 Corner Dumbarton Rd & Hyndland St, Partick) on the second and fourth Saturday of each month. There are plenty of tempting samples on offer, and traditional Scottish music adds to the atmosphere. There are also numerous delis in the city.

# Entertainment & nightlife

Glasgow is the hub of entertainment and nightlife in Scotland. As well as theatre and classical music, many of its live music, comedy venues and nightclubs have legendary status and keep the city buzzing year round. Whether you want to tap your feet to traditional Scottish music or dance until the early hours beneath flashing disco lights, you'll never be short of evening entertainment in the city.

Glaswegians are avid cinema-goers, hence the roaring success of the annual Glasgow Film Festival (see page 9), and the city boasts plenty of chain movie houses. However, there are also specialist cinemas. The **Glasgow Film Theatre** (ⓐ 12 Rose St ⓣ (0141) 332 6535 ⓦ www.gft.org.uk) is considered the finest cinema in Scotland and is the setting for independent films from around the world, as well as art-house movies. It's also one of the hosts of the annual Renault French Film Festival, celebrating new offerings from across the Channel. As part of the Science Centre, the **GSC IMAX cinema** (ⓐ Glasgow Science Centre, Pacific Quay ⓣ (0141) 420 5000) screens 3-D movies in digital sound. In addition, the city itself has contributed to the world of film by producing numerous international film stars, including Deborah Kerr, Robert Carlyle, John Hannah, David McCallum and James McAvoy.

As birthplace to one of Britain's most popular and successful comedians, Billy Connolly, it's not surprising that humour is a strong fixture on the Glasgow entertainment scene. There are dozens of regular venues and open-mic nights where budding comedians can try their hand with the inevitable hecklers, while stand-up comedy with professional comedians has been boosted even further by the Magners Glasgow International Comedy Festival (see page 12).

● *The GSC 3-D IMAX cinema is set in a stunning waterside location*

**WHAT'S ON**

Glasgow's main listings magazine (which also covers Edinburgh) is the weekly *The List*, available from the tourist office and most newsagents. As well as articles about events relevant to both cities, it gives full listings of club nights, cinemas, theatre, gay events and comedy. It is also online at ⓦ www.list.co.uk

**The Stand Comedy Club** (ⓐ 333 Woodlands Rd ⓣ 0870 600 6055 ⓦ www.thestand.co.uk) is an offshoot from its extremely popular branch in Edinburgh and is the most successful comedy venue in the city. There's also the **Jongleurs** (ⓐ Renfrew St ⓣ 0870 787 0707 ⓦ www.jongleurs.com) chain, which features both home-grown talents and touring well-known names.

The music scene is equally alive and kicking. Glasgow has given birth to innumerable bands that first gigged in their native city and went on to become international names. New talents regularly emerge from live music venues such as the legendary **King Tut's Wah Wah Hut** (ⓐ 272a St Vincent St ⓣ (0141) 221 5279) – where Oasis broke into the big time and where the emphasis is on indie music with a nod to rock, funk, punk and fusion. At the other end of the musical scale, acoustic folk is celebrated with regular sessions at venues such as **St Andrew's in the Square** (ⓐ 1 St Andrew's Square ⓣ (0141) 559 5902), a refurbished 18th-century church that hosts artists from a wide variety of genres. Large touring acts regularly play Glasgow's famous **Barrowland Ballroom** (ⓐ 244 Gallowgate ⓣ (0141) 552 4601 ⓦ www.glasgow-barrowland.com) or the **Glasgow Academy** (ⓐ 121 Eglinton St ⓣ (0141) 418 3000

Ⓦ www.glasgow-academy.co.uk) while big name stadium rock, featuring bands such as The Rolling Stones and Bon Jovi, is hewn at **Hampden Park**, Scotland's national stadium (ⓐ Hampden Park ⓘ (0141) 620 4000 Ⓦ www.hampdenpark.co.uk).

Glasgow is Scotland's clubbing capital and a range of clubs all over the city cater to all manner of tastes – from house to electronica to trance. Glasgow's gay district can be found in the Merchant City quarter.

🔴 *Hampden Park plays host to both sporting and musical events*

## Sport & relaxation

### SPECTATOR SPORTS
### Football

Football is almost a religion in Glasgow, and locals are split into Celtic fans and Rangers fans. Rivalries between football teams are common in all sporting nations, but the contest between Rangers and Celtic, known as the 'Old Firm', is fiercely heartfelt. In part this is due to religious sectarianism that remains strong throughout Glasgow – Celtic are a Catholic team; Rangers are Protestant. In recent years both teams have made efforts to remove the sectarian aspect from their game.

Celtic (in green and white) play at their home ground of **Celtic Park** (see page 90 for the Celtic Football Club Visitor Centre & Museum) and tickets to matches can be obtained either online at ⓦ www.celticfc.net or from the ticket office on ❶ 0871 226 1888. Rangers' (in blue and white) home ground is the **Ibrox Stadium** (see page 93 for the Rangers Football Club & Visitor Centre) and tickets there can be obtained by calling ❶ 0871 702 1972. Tickets, however, sell out very fast.

### Ice hockey
Having reached Scotland from Canada, ice hockey is now a popular spectator sport in Glasgow. The local team are the Paisley Pirates, and they ply their pucks at **Braehead Arena** (ⓐ Kings Inch Rd ❶ (0141) 886 8300).

### Rugby
The city's main rugby team is the Glasgow Warriors, who play at their home ground of **Firhill** (ⓐ 80 Firhill Rd ❶ Box office (0131) 346 5100).

## PARTICIPATION SPORTS
### Canoeing
Head out to Loch Lomond, where the company **Can You Experience?**
(📍 Loch Lomond Shores Visitor Centre, Balloch ☎ (01389) 756251
🌐 www.canyouexperience.com) organises both guided and
unguided canoe trips and equipment hire. What better way
to take in the breathtaking scenery of Britain's largest
inland waterway?

### Climbing
On Glasgow's Southside the **Glasgow Climbing Centre**
(📍 Ibrox Church, 534 Paisley Rd West ☎ (0141) 427 9550
🌐 www.glasgowclimbingcentre.co.uk) offers indoor rock climbing
within a converted church. Instruction is available for beginners,
and if you then want to do the real thing in the great outdoors
staff will give advice on the best places to go.

### Golf
There are more than 40 golf courses on the outskirts of Glasgow,
including the **World of Golf Centre** (📍 2700 Great Western Rd
☎ (0141) 944 4141) in the Clydebank area, which offers tuition,
floodlit ranges and a putting green.

### Skiing
Glasgow's **Xscape Braehead** (📍 Kings Inch Rd, Braehead, Renfrew
☎ 0871 200 3222 🌐 www.xscape.co.uk) boasts a 200 m (656 ft)
indoor slope, covered with over 1,700 tonnes of fresh snow. The
slope is suitable for both beginners (instructors are available)
and experienced skiers.

## Accommodation

Glasgow has accommodation to suit all budgets, from luxurious hotels to basic lodgings and from motels to quaint B&Bs both in and outside the city. Some hotels include breakfast in the room rate and some don't, so check before you book. In the larger hotels breakfast is likely to be a full Scottish affair, including black pudding and haggis.

Out of season it's not always necessary to book in advance, but this is a conference city so it's wise to check whether any major events are taking place at the time of your stay. The Scottish tourist board website (Ⓦ www.visitscotland.com) has a good accommodation search facility.

### HOTELS & GUEST HOUSES

**Babbity Bowster £** More famous for its downstairs bar (see page 74), the upstairs rooms in this 18th-century building are excellent value for money even if they're slightly lacking in amenities. ❸ 16–18 Blackfriars St (City Centre & Merchant City) ❶ (0141) 552 5055 Ⓝ Suburban railway: High Street

**Express by Holiday Inn £** No mod cons at all here – just a bed and a bathroom, but its central location makes it ideal for sightseeing

### PRICE CATEGORIES
The following ratings indicate the average price per double room per night. Some rooms may be more or less expensive than the rating suggests, depending on high or low season.
£ up to £60   ££ £60–150   £££ over £150

and bar-crawling. ⓐ Stockwell St (Southside & River Clyde)
ⓘ 0871 423 4876 ⓦ www.hiexpress.co.uk Ⓝ Subway: St Enoch

**Rennie Mackintosh City Hotel £** Set in a restored Victorian town house,
the décor here has been inspired by the ubiquitous designs of Charles
Rennie Mackintosh, making for a true Glaswegian atmosphere. It
also has the benefit of a garden – a rare thing in such a central
location. ⓐ 218–220 Renfrew St (City Centre & Merchant City)
ⓘ (0141) 333 9992 Ⓝ Suburban railway: Central; bus: 398, 505

**Brunswick Hotel ££** In the heart of Merchant City, this minimalist
boutique hotel is an ideal base if you're planning a night on the tiles.

🔺 *The stylish Rennie Mackintosh City Hotel*

ⓐ 106–108 Brunswick St (City Centre & Merchant City) ⓣ (0141) 552 0001
ⓦ www.brunswickhotel.co.uk ⓝ Suburban railway: Argyle Street

**Kirklee Hotel ££** If Glasgow's bustle gets too much for you, Kirklee
is the perfect antidote – in-room breakfast, a friendly lounge and
a rose garden belie the central position of this boutique hotel.
ⓐ 11 Kensington Gate (The West End) ⓣ (0141) 334 5555
ⓦ www.kirkleehotel.co.uk ⓝ Subway: Hillhead

**Malmaison ££** Set in a converted church, Malmaison is a chain hotel
that does away with the concept of chain hotels. It's stylish and
personable, with elegant rooms decorated in bold colours and a
champagne bar in the basement. ⓐ 278 West George St (City Centre
& Merchant City) ⓣ (0141) 572 1000 ⓦ www.malmaison-glasgow.com
ⓝ Suburban railway: Charing Cross

⬤ *All mod cons at the Radisson Blu*

**Radisson Blu ££** You won't feel pampered or special here, but if you want all the mod cons of a large chain hotel, as well as an indoor pool and spa facilities right in the centre of the city, you can't go wrong with the Radisson. ③ 301 Argylle St (City Centre & Merchant City) ① (0141) 204 3333 Ⓦ www.radissonblu.co.uk Ⓝ Subway: St Enoch

**Thistle Hotel ££** Conveniently situated in the heart of Glasgow's entertainment and shopping area, this comfortable hotel provides the ideal base from which to explore the city. ③ 36 Cambridge St (City Centre & Merchant City) ① 0871 376 9043 Ⓦ www.thistle.com Ⓝ Subway: Cowcaddens

**ABode Glasgow £££** Choose your room type by its title – Comfortable (at the cheaper end) to Fabulous (at top-price end), and Desirable and Enviable in between. ③ 129 Bath St (City Centre & Merchant City) ① (0141) 221 6789 Ⓦ www.abodehotels.co.uk Ⓝ Suburban railway: Queen Street; bus: 398, 505

**City Inn £££** A lovely place to take in the river views and ponder on the area's great shipbuilding history. ③ Finnieston Quay (Southside & River Clyde) ① (0141) 240 1002 Ⓦ www.cityinn.com Ⓝ Suburban railway: Exhibition Centre

**Hotel du Vin £££** This award-winning hotel provides the bed of choice for visiting celebrities and other wealthy guests, with its beautifully designed rooms all complete with wide-screen TVs. Despite this nod to modernity, however, the hotel's charm lies in its Victorian details, including stained-glass windows. ③ 1 Devonshire Gardens (The West End) ① (0141) 339 2001 Ⓦ www.hotelduvin.com Ⓝ Suburban railway: Hyndland

**Park Inn £££** If it's raining outside and you don't feel like sightseeing, you can always stay in your room and play with your joystick – yes, PlayStation is provided. The rooms themselves are all that one expects from luxury modern hotels – dark wood, crisp linen and contemporary art. There's also a spa and an on-site Pan-Asian restaurant. ➋ 2 Port Dundas Place (City Centre & Merchant City) ➊ (0141) 333 1500 Ⓦ www.glasgow.parkinn.co.uk Ⓝ Subway: Cowcaddens

### SELF-CATERING

For general information about Glasgow rental apartments see Ⓦ www.glasgowhotelsandapartments.co.uk

**Number 52 Charlotte Street ££** If you can't afford to live in a Georgian town house designed by Robert Adam, you can at least stay in one for a few days by renting one of these six serviced apartments. A cleaner comes daily to tidy and change linen, but breakfast is not included. ➋ 52 Charlotte St (City Centre & Merchant City) ➊ 0845 230 5252 Ⓦ www.52charlottestreet.co.uk Ⓝ Suburban railway: High Street

**The Spires ££** Wonderfully elegant central apartments, some of which have a terrace. ➋ The Pinnacle, 160 Bothwell St (City Centre & Merchant City) ➊ 0845 270 0090 Ⓦ www.thespires.co.uk Ⓝ Suburban railway: Charing Cross

**Fraser Suites Glasgow £££** A central 'aparthotel' – which means rooms with a kitchen and a general cleaner but no other facilities. Great for families or those who want a little more independence than a hotel offers. ➋ 1–19 Albion St (City Centre & Merchant City) ➊ (0141) 553 4288 Ⓦ www.frasersuitesglasgow.co.uk Ⓝ Suburban railway: High Street

## YOUTH HOSTELS

**Euro Hostel Glasgow £** There's a choice of single, double or dormitory accommodation here, with the added benefit that breakfast is included, but there's also a kitchen if you want to do your own thing. ⓐ 318 Clyde St (Southside & River Clyde) ⓣ (0141) 222 2828 ⓦ www.euro-hostels.co.uk ⓝ Suburban railway: Central; bus: 398, 505

**SY Hostel £** You need to be a member of the Youth Hostel Association to stay here, in dormitory rooms that sleep between four and six people. ⓐ 8 Park Terrace (The West End) ⓣ (0141) 332 3004 ⓦ www.syha.org.uk ⓝ Subway: St George's Cross

### CAMPING IT UP

The countryside around Glasgow, especially Loch Lomond (see page 118), makes for wonderful camping holidays in summer and all campsites are within easy reach of the city. Here's a selection:

**Cashel Camping & Caravan Park Balmaha** ⓐ Rowardennan, Glasgow ⓣ 0845 130 8224

**Clyde Valley Caravan Park** ⓐ Kirkfieldbank, Lanark ⓣ (01555) 663951

**Gart Caravan Park** ⓐ Stirling Rd, Callander ⓣ (01877) 330002

**Inverbeg Holiday Park** ⓐ Inverbeg, Luss ⓣ (01436) 860267

**Loch Lomond Holiday Park** ⓐ Loch Lomond, Inveruglas, Argyll ⓣ (01301) 704224 ⓦ www.lochlomond-lodges.co.uk

**Lomond Woods Holiday Park** ⓐ Balloch ⓣ (01389) 755000 ⓦ www.holiday-parks.co.uk

# THE BEST OF GLASGOW

As Glasgow stretches out before you, large, sprawling and irresistibly inviting, you may be overwhelmed by choice. Don't be. As the locals say, 'will ye no come back again?' Of course you will – you won't be able to stay away. What follows are ten suggestions for a love-at-first-visit jaunt.

## TOP 10 ATTRACTIONS

- **Kelvingrove Art Gallery & Museum** Glasgow's finest art collection includes works by Rembrandt and Constable, while the museum features a wonderful natural history section (see page 82)

- **Burrell Collection** More than 9,000 works of art from all over the world (see page 97)

- **Gallery of Modern Art** The finest collection of modern art in the city (see page 66)

- **The Barras** One of the most famous markets in Britain (see page 70)

- **Glasgow Cathedral** This medieval edifice dominates the cityscape, and the adjacent Necropolis is filled with impressive Victorian statuary (see page 60)

- **Charles Rennie Mackintosh** The master architect and designer left a distinctive mark on the city in places such as the Willow Tea Rooms. With a Mackintosh Trail Ticket you can explore many of his most outstanding works (see pages 68 & 20)

- **Pollok House** A wonderfully preserved Georgian house set within its own country park – in which you'll also find the famed Burrell Collection (see pages 92 & 97)

- **Glasgow Science Centre** Built for the Millennium, the science centre includes hands-on exhibits and a planetarium (see page 92)

- **Scottish Football Museum** Everything you ever wanted to know about Scotland's contribution to the 'beautiful game' (see page 100)

- **Magners Glasgow International Comedy Festival** One of Glasgow's annual highlights, as venues all over the town host international comedians (see page 12)

🔻 *Kelvingrove Art Gallery & Museum*

## Suggested itineraries

### HALF-DAY: GLASGOW IN A HURRY

If you're only in Glasgow on a business trip or just passing through but have time for a little exploration, head straight for the city centre quadrant of Buchanan Street and Argyle Street. There you can spend an hour or so in the Gallery of Modern Art (see page 66) and then indulge in some top class retail therapy in Princes Square (see page 72).

### 1 DAY: TIME TO SEE A LITTLE MORE

If you have more than half a day, head slightly east to take in the looming glory of Glasgow Cathedral (see page 60). Soak up the atmosphere of Merchant City (see page 62), once home to tobacco magnates and now a trendy area of bars and restaurants, then enjoy the rambling atmosphere of The Barras market – a Glasgow institution (see page 70).

🔻 *Glasgow Science Centre*

## 2–3 DAYS: TIME TO SEE MUCH MORE

With more time on your hands, don't miss an opportunity to visit the Kelvingrove Art Gallery & Museum (see page 82), with one of the finest art collections in the country. For a step back in time, visit the Museum of Transport (see page 83) to see how Glaswegians got around in days gone by. Head to the Southside of the city for the gleaming success that is the Glasgow Science Centre (see page 92) and take in the views of the Clyde riverbank. Then visit the Burrell Collection (see page 97) and stroll around Pollok Park (see page 92).

## LONGER: ENJOYING GLASGOW TO THE FULL

With added time you can revisit some of the areas to take in more hidden sights, such as the Glasgow School of Art with its Rennie Mackintosh designs (see page 68) or the historic Tall Ship on the Clyde (see page 94). But don't miss the chance to get out into the countryside, particularly Loch Lomond (see page 118), one of the most picturesque areas of Scotland.

# Something for nothing

Glasgow is not an expensive place to visit – at least no more so than any other British city, and considerably less so than most. Additionally, many of the museums and galleries are free, although there may be charges for special temporary exhibitions.

When Glasgow was considerably expanded during the 19th century, the city planners had the foresight and consideration to include large pockets of greenery in their aims. As a result it has far more parks and gardens than the majority of cities that were created and developed during the Industrial Revolution. The Botanic Gardens (see page 78) are the highlight, but Pollok Country Park (see page 92) and Bellahouston Park (see page 90) also make for lovely strolls, providing the skies are clear. Should rain stop play when you are visiting Glasgow Green, you can duck into the People's Palace exhibition (see page 64) for a (free) potted history of the city. On the Southside, what was once a derelict industrial site now holds the peaceful **Hidden Gardens** (🄰 Albert Drive ☏ (0141) 433 2722 🌐 www.thehiddengardens.org.uk 🕓 10.00–20.00 Tues–Sat, 12.00–18.00 Sun, May–Sept; 10.00–16.00 Tues–Sat, 12.00–16.00 Sun, Oct–Apr), with their themes of spirituality and contemplation.

The Victorians had a macabre fascination with death, and many 19th-century cemeteries are adorned with ornate neo-Gothic statuary. Glasgow's necropolis (see page 60) has an abundance of florid mausoleums, tombs and gravestones. One can't help admire the skill of the sculptors and you can lose yourself for hours strolling around these flamboyant celebrations of past lives.

When the Clyde was still the centre of industry and shipbuilding this was a bustling area, and a few remnants of that time remain – such as the Finnieston Crane, which was used to lift large cargoes onto the ships. Nowadays it's uplifting to see how the area is being regenerated, especially with the Pacific Quay development that's linked to the city centre by the Clyde Arc bridge. A number of attractions, including The Tall Ship (see page 94), the Clydebuilt Scottish Maritime Museum (see page 98) and the Scottish Exhibition & Conference Centre (see page 94), are also based here.

🔺 *The People's Palace*

# When it rains

Lucky indeed the visitor to Glasgow who doesn't experience a spot of wet weather. The city's rainy reputation is well founded and the likelihood is that you'll experience more than a few showers, if not a full-on downpour. Going out without an umbrella or a hat is foolhardy, to say the least.

That said, the city is also awash with fascinating museums that should keep you dry and enthralled for days. The Kelvingrove Art Gallery & Museum (see page 82) and the Burrell Collection (see page 97) both warrant several hours of attention, while the many buildings dedicated to Charles Rennie Mackintosh, such as the Glasgow School of Art (see page 68) and Mackintosh House in the Hunterian Art Gallery (see page 82), are must-sees that are also protected from the elements. If you've got kids in tow, they will be absorbed for hours by the interactive exhibits at the Glasgow Science Centre (see page 92).

Partly because of the weather conditions, Glasgow is also very strong on shopping centres. The most elegant of these is Princes Square (see page 72) with its four floors of chic boutiques and ground-floor cafés and restaurants. If you've got a bit more cash in your wallet and crave a European experience to combat the Scottish climate, don't miss The Italian Centre (see page 70), which brings a spot of Mediterranean sparkle to the grey skies.

Indoor sporting options include putting your foot down at **Scotkart** go-karting track (ⓣ (0141) 641 0222 ⓦ www.scotkart.co.uk). Or, if you're gastronomically inclined, the **Glasgow Cookery School** (ⓐ 65 Glassford St ⓣ (0141) 552 5239 ⓦ www.thecookeryschool.org) offers one-day courses on all manner of cuisines, including Scottish. What an opportunity to nail that haggis recipe.

Of course, this being Scotland you're never more than a few steps from a pub, where a pint of ale and a hearty meat pie can do wonders to lift the spirits if the heavens have decided to open. Let it rain!

⬥ *An ancient archway leads to exhibits in the Burrell Collection*

# On arrival

### TIME DIFFERENCE

Glasgow's clocks follow Greenwich Mean Time (GMT). During Daylight Saving Time (end Mar–end Oct) the clocks are put forward one hour.

### ARRIVING

### By air

**Glasgow International Airport** (ⓐ Abbotsinch, Paisley ① (0141) 848 4769 ⓦ www.glasgowairport.com) is just 12 km (8 miles) from the city centre. The efficient Glasgow Flyer Airport Express bus connects the two for the 20-minute journey. There are also plenty of taxis available. For details of national and international flights landing at Glasgow, see page 144.

If you arrive at **Glasgow Prestwick International Airport** (ⓐ Prestwick ① 0871 223 0700 ⓦ www.gpia.co.uk), 48 km (30 miles) from the city centre, you'll find there are train services every half an hour to Glasgow Central Station and regular bus services to Buchanan Bus Station.

### By rail

There are two main train stations in Glasgow: **Central Station** on Gordon Street serves trains to the south and west; **Queen Street Station** on Dundas Street serves trains to the north and east. Train services into Glasgow are handled by East Coast, Virgin and First ScotRail. There are daily services between London and Glasgow making the four and a half to five and a half-hour journey, as well as direct links to many other British cities. For timetables and fares contact **National Rail Enquiries** (① 0845 748 4950 ⓦ www.nationalrail.co.uk).

## By road

**National Express** coaches (☎ 0870 580 8080
🌐 www.nationalexpress.com) link Glasgow with various UK and
Scottish cities and are a great budget option. The main bus station
is **Buchanan Bus Station** (📧 174 Buchanan St ☎ (0141) 353 2141).

⬇ *This ornate building is now the Travel Centre in St Enoch*

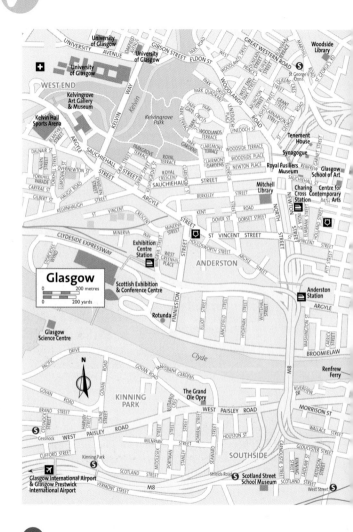

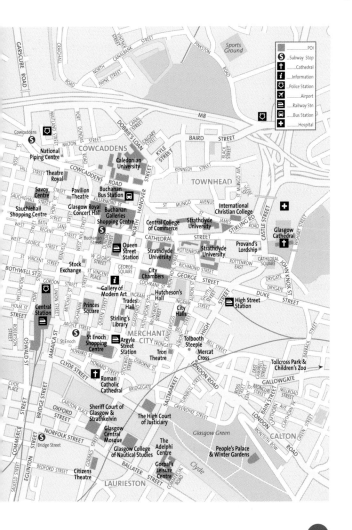

POI
S ...Subway Stop
✝ ...Cathedral
ℹ ...Information
👮 ...Police Station
✈ ...Airport
🚆 ...Railway Stn
🚌 ...Bus Station
✚ ...Hospital

Sports Ground

GARSCUBE ROAD

M8

COWCADDENS

National Piping Centre

Cowcaddens S

TOWNHEAD

Theatre Royal

Savoy Centre

Sauchiehall Shopping Centre

Pavilion Theatre

Caledonian University

Buchanan Bus Station

Glasgow Royal Concert Hall

Buchanan Galleries Shopping Centre

Central College of Commerce

International Christian College

Strathclyde University

Glasgow Cathedral

Stock Exchange

Queen Street Station

Strathclyde University

Strathclyde University

Provand's Lordship

Central Station

Gallery of Modern Art

City Chambers

Trades' Hall

Hutcheson's Hall

High Street Station

Princes Square

Stirling's Library

City Halls

Argyle Street Station

St Enoch Shopping Centre

St Enoch S

MERCHANT CITY

Tron Theatre

Tolbooth Steeple

Mercat Cross

Tollcross Park & Children's Zoo

GALLOWGATE

Roman Catholic Cathedral

Bridge Street

Sheriff Court of Glasgow & Strathkelvin

The High Court of Justiciary

Glasgow Green

CALTON

Glasgow Central Mosque

Glasgow College of Nautical Studies

The Adelphi Centre

People's Palace & Winter Gardens

Citizens Theatre

Gorbal's Leisure Centre

LAURIESTON

The main motorway route into Glasgow is the M6/M74, which travels up the west of England, through Cumbria. The city is directly linked to Edinburgh via the M8. The journey time by road between London and Glasgow is about nine hours.

## FINDING YOUR FEET

Glasgow is generally a safe city as long as you're in the central tourist areas, so no visitor should feel any sense of threat. Like everywhere, in crowded tourist spots pickpockets may be in operation so keep an eye on your belongings at all times. Traffic can be a problem in the centre so use the pedestrian crossings, wait for the green man to light up and remember that traffic will be coming from the right. Police, taxi drivers and locals, who have a well-founded reputation for being friendly, will all help if you need to ask for directions.

## ORIENTATION

Glasgow is a large city so it's best to arm yourself with a map, available free from the tourist office (see page 152). The main areas for tourists are the city centre (see page 60), Merchant City (see page 62), the West End (see page 78) and the Southside (see page 90). The central axes of the city centre are the interconnecting Sauchiehall, Buchanan and Argyle streets. Exploring on foot within each area is the best option, but for travelling around the bus service is excellent, the subway system links the city centre and the West End, and taxis are plentiful. There's also an extensive train network for more outlying districts.

⏵ *A statue of one of Scotland's heroes, Robert the Bruce*

## GETTING AROUND

There is an extensive bus network in Glasgow operated by **First**
(☎ (0141) 636 3215 🌐 www.firstgroup.com). Glass sheltered bus stops
are in abundance and will have a plan of the route each numbered
bus will take. Selected stops on the route are also written on the
front of the bus. Single-day bus passes are available or you can pay
for single fares, but you must have the exact change. Fares start
from 90p for a short single journey in the city centre. The main
bus station in Glasgow is on Buchanan Street (see page 49) in the

🔺 *Hop On Hop Off around the city*

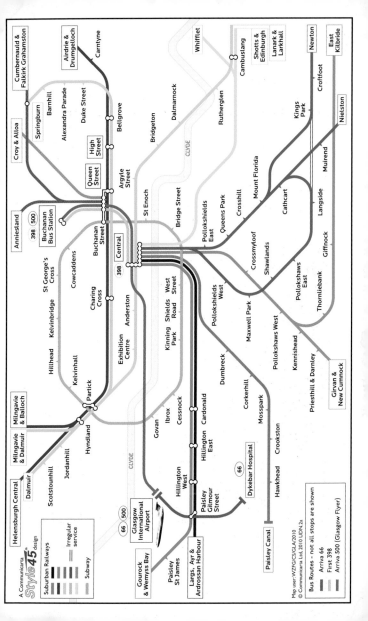

city centre, from where you can take buses around the city, and to many other places around Scotland.

Glasgow's subway is the third-oldest subway system in the world. Single tickets or day or weekly passes can be bought at station ticket offices or, with the correct change, at the ticket machines. For more information contact **Strathclyde Passenger Transport (SPT)** (☎ (0141) 332 6811 🌐 www.spt.co.uk).

Where venues in the city centre of Glasgow are listed in this guide without public transport practical information, you can assume that they are most easily reached on foot or by taxi.

Black cabs are in plentiful supply on Glasgow's streets and can be hailed from the pavement if their yellow For Hire light is on. Most taxi drivers are friendly and helpful and love to talk about their city with tourists. Fares are metered and the cost is shown on a light above the driver's windscreen. At the end of your journey pay the driver through the glass cavity between the driver's and passenger's compartment. The limit of passengers per taxi is five people. There are also various companies that you can telephone to order a taxi from your location, including:

**Glasgow Taxis** ☎ (0141) 429 7070

**Online Radio Cars** ☎ (0141) 550 4040

Traffic can be heavy in the city and parking is restricted, so driving is not the most sensible option. If you do want to drive, however, make sure you understand the parking regulations, use pay and display ticket machines or one of the multi-storey car parks, and never park on double yellow lines or red routes. Traffic wardens abound and are very keen on writing tickets.

---

▶ *The many bridges over the River Clyde make for an interesting walk*

If you're just coming into Glasgow for the day, en route to other destinations, there is a useful 'Park and Ride' scheme, where you can park your car on the outskirts of the city and take a bus into the centre. Locations of the many 'Park and Ride' stops are indicated on the city's transport map, available from the tourist office, the bus station and mainline stations.

## CAR HIRE

Hiring a car certainly isn't necessary if you are just going to explore the city. However, it can be a very convenient way to get around if you plan to visit outlying areas. As well as multinational chains such as Avis and Hertz, there are several Glasgow-based car-hire options. Costs obviously vary between companies, but the average for an economy size car is £30 for a day and £150 for a week's hire. Some reputable companies are:

**Avis** ☏ 0844 544 6064 ⓦ www.avis.co.uk
**Clarkson of Scotland** ☏ (0141) 771 3990 ⓦ www.carhirescotland.com
**Hertz** ☏ 0870 850 2657 ⓦ www.hertz.co.uk
**Thrifty Car Rental** ☏ (0141) 248 3868 ⓦ www.thrifty.co.uk

▶ *Kelvingrove Park*

 THE CITY OF
Glasgow

# City Centre & Merchant City

Glasgow's city centre may not have the trendy reputation of its West End (on the other side of the M8 that cuts through the city, see page 78), but it is where the action is in terms of administration, business and high-street shopping. Glasgow was founded on the site of its cathedral, so this is the true heart of the city both historically and financially. Much of Glasgow's wealth emerged in the 18th and 19th centuries, when the importation of tobacco from the New World created rich magnates who built their homes and warehouses in the area now known as Merchant City. Today, these glorious edifices have been given over to shops and restaurants that have helped boost Glasgow's fortunes once again.

## SIGHTS & ATTRACTIONS

### City Chambers
The 19th century was the heyday of Glasgow's history and this striking building reflects the success of the time with its marble staircases and frescoed ceilings. Glasgow City Council still operates from behind the majestic façade, which dominates George Square.
ⓐ George Square ⓣ (0141) 287 4018 ⓦ www.glasgow.gov.uk
ⓛ Tours: 10.30 & 14.30 Mon–Fri ⓥ Bus: 398

### Glasgow Cathedral & Necropolis
Dating from the 12th century, this is one of the city's most impressive buildings and is the lone mainland survivor of the Scottish Reformation of the 16th century. Its most important feature is the shrine of St Mungo, the first bishop of Strathclyde and the patron saint of Glasgow. The Necropolis next to the cathedral only

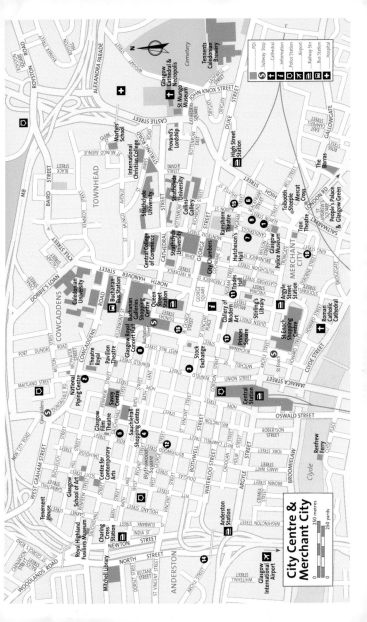

# City Centre & Merchant City

dates from the 19th century but is full of Gothic-style mausoleums for many Glasgow notables (including William Miller, author of the children's nursery rhyme 'Wee Willie Winkie'). ⓐ Castle St ⓘ (0141) 552 8198 ⓦ www.glasgow-cathedral.com ⓛ 09.30–18.00 Mon–Sat, 13.00–17.00 Sun, Apr–Sept; 09.30–16.30 Mon–Sat, 13.00–16.00 Sun, Oct–Mar ⓝ Suburban railway: High Street

## Martyrs' School

When primary education became compulsory in the late 19th century, the country was involved in a mass project of school building. This primary school, built in 1897, was one of Charles Rennie Mackintosh's earliest works; nevertheless his distinctive style can still be seen in the tiling and woodwork. Following conventions of the time, there are separate entrances for boys and girls, with classrooms radiating out from the central hall. You will have to admire it from the outside, since it is now used by the staff of Glasgow Museums and is not open for visiting. ⓐ Parson St, off Glebe St ⓘ (0141) 553 2557 ⓦ www.glasgowmuseums.com ⓝ Bus: X8, X8A

## Merchant City

A huge influence on the rise of Glasgow's fortunes in the 18th century was the importing of tobacco, and it is in this region of the city centre that the great tobacco magnates built their warehouses and opulent homes. Like many industrial areas in Britain, the area fell into disrepair in the 20th century, but in the 1980s a rejuvenation programme was put in place to preserve the architecture and revive its fortunes. One of the most successful ventures was Ingram Square, where derelict warehouses were converted into chic apartments, shops and cafés.

▶ *Victorian statuary at the Necropolis*

Other buildings of note in the area include Hutcheson's Hall (1802) on Ingram Street; the Greek Revivalist Sheriff Courts (1842), also on Ingram Street and now home to the Scottish Youth Theatre; the City Halls (1882) on Candleriggs; the original Tolbooth (1625) at The Cross; the Britannia Music Hall (1857) on Trongate (where Cary Grant once performed); the Virginia Galleries (1819); the former Tobacco Exchange on Virginia Street; and the Corinthian (1841) at the top of South Frederick Street. So important is the area now to the city's history that Glasgow Council have put in place a Merchant City trail.
Ⓦ www.glasgowmerchantcity.net Ⓢ Suburban railway: Argyle Street

**People's Palace & Glasgow Green**
Glasgow Green was a grazing land in medieval times and also served as a horse market – a history still commemorated by the annual Glasgow Fair held here each July. Within the green is a memorial to the inventor James Watt, who is said to have figured out his steam engine mechanisms while taking a stroll here. The People's Palace was opened in 1898 and is now home to a museum dedicated to Glasgow's history and its people – there are re-creations of a prison cell here, displays about Clyde steamers and, quirkily, the banana boots that comedian Billy Connolly wore during the documentary Big Banana Feet, which was to make his name. The glasshouse next door is home to an array of tropical plants as well as a café.
Ⓐ Glasgow Green Ⓣ (0141) 276 2788 Ⓞ 10.00–17.00 Mon–Thur & Sat, 11.00–17.00 Fri & Sun Ⓥ Bus: 16, 18, 40, 61, 62, 64, 263

**Provand's Lordship**
Since Glasgow burst into prominence during the Industrial Revolution, it's sometimes hard to remember that people were living here centuries beforehand. This, the only surviving medieval house in the city, is proof

of its long history, dating from 1471. Inside is a collection of historic furniture and exhibitions detailing life in the city in the Middle Ages. ⓐ Castle St ⓣ (0141) 552 8819 ⓦ www.glasgowmuseums.com ⓛ 10.00–17.00 Mon–Thur & Sat, 11.00–17.00 Fri & Sun ⓝ Bus: X1, X14, X67

### Tenement House

Tenement living is central to Glasgow's history, as much as it is to New York's. In this tenement building, one flat of four rooms has been preserved in the manner in which it was lived in by one resident for five decades from 1911 until 1965, detailing the history of tenement living and domestic life in the early 20th century. There's also a general exhibition on life in the tenements. ⓐ Buccleuch St ⓣ (0141) 333 0183 ⓦ www.nts.org.uk ⓛ 13.00–17.00 Mar–Oct ⓝ Subway: Cowcaddens. Admission charge

### Trades Hall

This lovely 18th-century building designed by the great architect Robert Adam was home to the trading body that was responsible for training craftsmen. Today it houses an audio exhibition on the history of the city, from medieval times to the present day. ⓐ Glassford St ⓣ (0141) 552 2418 ⓦ www.tradeshallglasgow.co.uk ⓛ 10.00–16.00 Mon–Fri, 09.00–12.00 Sat; tours: 10.00 Tues ⓝ Suburban railway: Argyle Street. Admission charge

## CULTURE

### Centre for Contemporary Arts (CCA)

Contemporary visual exhibits in the centre of town by local, national and international artists. There's an atrium café and shop, Jorge Pardo-designed bar serving snacks all day, and a huge events programme.

ⓐ 350 Sauchiehall St ⓣ (0141) 352 4900 ⓦ www.cca-glasgow.com
ⓛ 11.00–18.00 Tues–Sat ⓝ Suburban railway: Charing Cross

### Collins Gallery

Ten annual exhibitions are staged in the University of Strathclyde's
gallery in all manner of contemporary genres – multimedia, applied
art and installations have all been seen here. Workshops are also
held. ⓐ Richmond St ⓣ (0141) 548 2558 ⓦ www.strath.ac.uk
ⓛ 10.00–17.00 Mon–Fri, 12.00–16.00 Sat ⓝ Suburban railway:
High Street

### Gallery of Modern Art

If you were ever in doubt of the wealth of Glasgow's tobacco
merchants, take a look at the façade of the Gallery of Modern Art –
it was once the private residence of one such magnate. The building
became the city's Royal Exchange before being converted into an art
gallery spanning the post-war period to the present day. ⓐ Royal
Exchange Square ⓣ (0141) 287 3050 ⓦ www.glasgowmuseums.com
ⓛ 10.00–17.00 Mon–Wed & Sat, 10.00–20.00 Thur, 11.00–17.00 Fri
& Sun ⓝ Suburban railway: Argyle Street

### Glasgow Police Museum

Glasgow was the first British city to have a police force and this
museum details its history from its beginnings in 1779. Truncheons,
handcuffs, uniforms, whistles, helmets and all manner of other
police paraphernalia are featured here. There is also an exhibition
dedicated to police uniforms from around the world. ⓐ Bell St
ⓣ (0141) 552 1818 ⓦ www.policemuseum.org.uk ⓛ 10.00–16.30
Mon–Sat, 12.00–16.30 Sun, Apr–Oct; 10.00–16.30 Tues, 12.00–16.30
Sun, Nov–Mar ⓝ Suburban railway: Argyle Street

● *Glasgow's Gallery of Modern Art*

## Glasgow School of Art

Although this is still an ongoing learning institution bustling with students hoping to be the next bright young thing on the art scene, the importance of the building as a Charles Rennie Mackintosh masterpiece means that guided tours are held here. Mackintosh designed the building in 1896, including a façade that is dominated

### CHARLES RENNIE MACKINTOSH

No other architect or designer has had such an effect on Glasgow's landscape in quite such an attractive manner as Charles Rennie Mackintosh. Born in the city in 1868, Mackintosh studied at the old Glasgow School of Art as well as working as an apprentice architect, and began to merge the two previously very different design forms into one. Taking inspiration from the Art Nouveau and Arts and Crafts movements that were sweeping across Europe and North America, Mackintosh fused Scottish symbolism into these forms with motifs such as his trademark rose. Other typical features of his design include the use of monochrome (black and white) colour schemes, high-backed geometric-shaped chairs and curved lamps. One of his most famous works, aside from the Glasgow School of Art (see above), is the Willow Tea Rooms (see page 74). Commissioned by his unofficial patron Catherine Cranston, who wanted to open a new dining emporium, Mackintosh mixed grey silk with purple velvet, and adorned the elegant area with chandeliers and glass doors. He also installed a window running along the full width of the room – an unusual feature at the time. He died in London in 1928. Ⓦ www.crmsociety.com

by huge windows, bringing vast amounts of light into the art studios. Inside is the beautiful wood-panelled library and collections from the artist's body of work, including sketches and furniture. ⓐ Renfrew St ⓣ (0141) 353 4500 ⓦ www.gsa.ac.uk ⓛ Tours: 10.30–14.30 Apr–Sept; 11.00 & 14.00 Mon–Fri, 10.30 & 11.30 Sat, Oct–Mar ⓝ Subway: Cowcaddens. Admission charge

## National Piping Centre

There's no sound quite so reminiscent of Scotland than the bagpipes, and this museum traces the history of the instrument and Highland music, with various sets of pipes from different periods. There's also a piping school where you can try your hand at playing the notoriously difficult instrument yourself in either day or evening classes. ⓐ McPhater St ⓣ (0141) 353 0220 ⓦ www.thepipingcentre.co.uk ⓛ 09.30–16.30 Mon–Fri; also open 09.00–13.00 Sat, 10.00–16.00 Sun, May–Sept ⓝ Subway: Cowcaddens. Admission charge

## Royal Highland Fusiliers Museum

Those interested in military history will have their fill here, as the museum records the history of the Scottish regiment through documents, uniforms and other military artefacts. ⓐ Sauchiehall St ⓣ (0141) 332 5639 ⓦ www.rhf.org.uk ⓛ 09.00–17.00 Mon–Fri ⓝ Subway: Cowcaddens

## St Mungo Museum of Religious Life & Art

St Mungo may be the Christian patron saint of Glasgow, but this museum celebrates tolerance by bringing together exhibits on the six major religious faiths of the world – Christianity, Judaism, Islam, Buddhism, Hinduism and Sikhism. There's even a Zen

garden, exuding Buddhist harmony. ⓐ Castle St ⓣ (0141) 276 1625
ⓦ www.glasgowmuseums.com ⓛ 10.00–17.00 Mon–Thur & Sat,
11.00–17.00 Fri & Sun ⓝ Suburban railway: High Street

## RETAIL THERAPY

**The Barras** One of the most authentic pockets of Glasgow, this
indoor and outdoor market has an eclectic collection of knick-knacks,
genuine antiques and, frankly, rubbish. But the atmosphere and the
market characters are what make this such a memorable experience.
ⓐ Gallowgate ⓛ 10.00–17.00 Sat & Sun

**Buchanan Galleries** One of Glasgow's newest shopping centres and
proving a great success, not least on account of its location. Standard
high-street stores such as Mango and Gap can be found here, as
well as a branch of John Lewis. ⓐ 220 Buchanan St ⓣ (0141) 333 9898
ⓦ www.buchanangalleries.co.uk ⓛ 09.00–18.00 Mon–Wed & Fri,
09.00–20.00 Thur, 09.00–19.00 Sat, 10.00–18.00 Sun

**Firework Studios** No rockets or Catherine wheels here – 'firework'
refers to the process by which they produce original ceramic
designs. The centre also runs pottery workshops if you want to
try your hand at it yourself. ⓐ 35A Dalhousie St ⓣ (0141) 332 3738
ⓦ www.fireworksceramics.co.uk ⓛ Hours vary, so phone to check

**The Italian Centre** Italy has long been known as a leader in design,
and this unique centre promotes the very best that the country has
to offer in designer clothing and accessories, including branches of
Armani and Versace. In addition there are plenty of cafés and bars if
you want to rest your feet and ponder your purchases. ⓐ 7 John St

🛈 (0141) 552 6099 🕒 10.00–18.00 Mon–Wed, Fri & Sat, 10.00–19.00 Thur, 12.00–17.00 Sun

**Merchant Square** Every Saturday, the square is home to a craft and designers market that is perennially popular with locals and visitors. ⓐ Candleriggs 🕒 11.30–18.00 Sat

🔺 *Interior of the Merchant Square market*

**Orro Contemporary Jewellery** In the heart of Merchant City this is a wonderful collection of modern jewellery from some of the world's best-known designers. 🅐 12 Wilson St 🕿 (0141) 552 7888 🌐 www.orro.co.uk 🕐 11.00–17.30 Tues–Sat

**Princes Square** The most elegant place to shop in the city – with everything under one roof. Behind an innocuous looking façade, the interior opens out to reveal a four-storey emporium of upmarket shops and designer one-offs, fountains and restaurants. 🅐 48 Buchanan St 🕿 (0141) 221 0324 🌐 www.princessquare.co.uk 🕐 09.30–18.00 Mon–Wed & Fri, 09.30–20.00 Thur, 09.00–18.00 Sat, 12.00–17.00 Sun

**St Enoch Shopping Centre** This may be the largest glass building in Europe, but the shopping centre within lacks any finesse. Still, it's good for families as it has a play centre, and it's useful for picking up everyday items from high-street chains. 🅐 55 St Enoch Square 🕿 (0141) 204 3900 🌐 www.stenoch.co.uk 🕐 09.00–18.00 Mon–Wed, 09.00–20.00 Thur, 09.00–18.00 Fri & Sat, 11.00–17.30 Sun

**Slanj Kiltmakers** If you're after a bit of traditional tartan or Highland gear, this is the place to come. 🅐 166 Hope St 🕿 (0141) 248 7770 🌐 www.slanjkilts.com 🕐 09.30–17.30 Mon–Sat

## TAKING A BREAK

**Café Gandolfi £ ❶** A Merchant City favourite with a stunning interior of stained glass and wood. Snacks and more substantial dishes are both available. 🅐 64 Albion St 🕿 (0141) 552 6813 🌐 www.cafegandolfi.com 🕐 09.00–23.30 Mon–Sat, 12.00–23.30 Sun

▲ *The Princes Square shopping centre has style both inside and out*

**Café Hula £ ❷** Homemade soup, enormous sandwiches and fresh cakes make this an ideal lunch spot in the city centre. ⓐ 321 Hope St ❶ (0141) 353 1660 ⓦ www.cafehula.co.uk ❶ 08.00–20.00 Mon–Wed, 08.00–21.00 Thur, 08.00–22.00 Fri & Sat, 11.00–18.00 Sun

**Fratelli Sarti £ ❸** Specialising in Tuscan cuisine, the café of this well-known deli has a superb selection of antipasti – ideal for a lunchtime snack. ⓐ 42 Renfield St ❶ (0141) 572 7000 ⓦ www.sarti.co.uk ❶ 08.00–00.00 Mon–Fri, 10.00–00.00 Sat, 12.30–00.00 Sun

**Where the Monkey Sleeps £–££ ❹** An achingly trendy café with a quirky interior and a menu of bagels, paninis and salads. ⓐ 182 West Regent St ❶ (0141) 226 3406 ⓦ www.monkeysleeps.com ❶ 07.00–17.00 Mon–Fri, 10.00–17.00 Sat

**Willow Tea Rooms £–££ ❺** Charles Rennie Mackintosh's beautifully designed tea rooms were originally opened in 1903 and have recently been refurbished. There are few more elegant and historic places in which to enjoy a slice of cake and a cup of tea in the heart of the city's shopping district. ⓐ 217 Sauchiehall St ❶ (0141) 332 0521 ⓦ www.willowtearooms.co.uk ❶ 09.00–17.00 Mon–Sat, 11.00–16.00 Sun

## AFTER DARK

## RESTAURANTS
**Babbity Bowster £ ❻** Set in a lovely 18th-century building originally built by Robert Adam and restored in the 1980s' regeneration of Merchant City, this is one of Glasgow's most perennially popular pubs. There's also a restaurant on the first floor, and a small hotel

above that (see page 34). 🅐 16–18 Blackfriars St 🕾 (0141) 552 5055 🕒 12.00–22.00 Mon–Sat, 12.30–22.00 Sun

**Dakhin £ ❼** Southern Indian curries are the speciality here in what many consider one of the best Indian restaurants in the city. 🅐 89 Candleriggs 🕾 (0141) 553 2585 🕸 www.dakhin.com 🕒 12.00–14.00, 17.00–22.30 Mon–Thur, 12.00–14.00, 17.00–23.00 Fri, 13.00–23.00 Sat & Sun

**O Sole Mio £ ❽** This classic Italian restaurant has an authentic trattoria feel with tables separated by wooden trellises. The food is excellent. 🅐 34–36 Bath St 🕾 (0141) 331 1397 🕒 12.00–14.30, 17.00–23.00 Mon–Sat, 17.00–23.00 Sun

**Arta ££ ❾** Set in what was once the city cheese market, this elegant Mediterranean restaurant, with an emphasis on both Spanish and Italian cuisine, benefits from an interior courtyard and a large bar. There's also a club on the premises on Friday and Saturday nights. 🅐 The Old Cheesemarket, 62 Albion St 🕾 0845 166 6018 🕸 www.g1group.co.uk 🕒 17.00–21.30 Wed & Thur, 17.00–23.00 Fri & Sun

**Café Cossachok ££ ❿** Glasgow's only Russian restaurant has been drawing crowds for almost two decades. As well as Russian fare such as beef stroganoff and *pelemni* (a type of ravioli), there are more than 40 brands of vodka on offer and, on Sundays, traditional Russian folk music. In addition, the staff wear traditional costume and the décor is an eclectic mix of Russian knick-knacks. 🅐 10 King St 🕾 (0141) 553 0733 🕸 www.cossachok.com 🕒 11.30–23.00 Mon–Thur, 16.00–23.00 Fri & Sun

**Corinthian ££** ⓫ Following a major refurbishment, this perennially popular restaurant also includes a nightclub, casino and cocktail bar. ⓐ 191 Ingram St ⓣ (0141) 552 1101 ⓦ www.thecorinthianclub.co.uk ⓛ 17.00–22.30 Mon-Fri, 12.00–22.30 Sat, 17.00–21.30 Sun

**Gamba ££** ⓬ If you're a lover of seafood this is one of the best Glasgow options. It gets busy so it's wise to book. ⓐ 225a West George St ⓣ (0141) 572 0899 ⓛ 12.00–14.30, 17.00–22.30

**Rogano ££** ⓭ The seafood menu, including oysters, is reflected in the décor of this well-known restaurant, decorated in the style of the luxury Queen Mary cruise liner. ⓐ 11 Exchange Place, off Buchanan St ⓣ (0141) 248 4055 ⓛ 12.00–14.30, 18.30–23.00

🔺 For unusual décor with your oysters, try Rogano

**The Buttery £££** ⓴ The oldest restaurant in Glasgow, established in 1856, is set in an old tenement building and still serves excellent Scottish cuisine. You'd do well to dress smartly and book ahead. ⓐ 652 Argyle St ⓣ (0141) 221 8188 ⓛ 12.00–15.00, 17.30–22.30 Mon–Sat, 12.30–21.00 Sun

**Qua £££** ⓯ A top Italian restaurant nestled in Glasgow's Merchant City area and a short walk from some of the best bars and clubs the city has to offer. ⓐ 68 Ingram St ⓣ (0141) 552 6233 ⓛ 12.00–22.00

**Windows £££** ⓰ Enjoy wonderful views of the city while dining on top-quality Scottish fare in the rooftop restaurant of the Carlton George Hotel. ⓐ 44 West George St ⓣ (0141) 354 5070 ⓦ www.carltonhotels.co.uk ⓛ 12.00–14.30, 17.00–21.45 Mon–Fri, 12.30–14.30, 17.00–21.45 Sat & Sun

## BARS & CLUBS

**Bar 91** This stylish bar typifies the regeneration of the Merchant City area. In the evening there is music from a DJ. ⓐ 91 Candleriggs ⓣ (0141) 552 5211 ⓛ 11.00–00.00

**Nice 'n' Sleazy** If you're into indie music, try this Sauchiehall Street institution, where nightly gigs take place in the basement while the ground floor rocks to the city's most eclectic jukebox. ⓐ 421 Sauchiehall St ⓣ (0141) 333 0900 ⓦ www.nicensleazy.com ⓛ 12.00–03.00

# The West End

The West End is the trendiest area of Glasgow today. However, until the middle of the 19th century there was little here at all bar a few mansions for the wealthy who appreciated the 'country' atmosphere. But the Industrial Revolution changed all that. With the city centre given over to enterprise it had also become unbearably crowded and dirty, and it was clear that land would have to be developed to house the growing number of residents of this burgeoning city. The formerly rural district to the west began to see a building boom of terraces and tenements, constructed from local sandstone, with particular care taken to ensure that parks and gardens, such as Kelvingrove, were also thrown into the mix. These were to be the new homes of the equally newly created middle classes.

Among the architects to contribute to this project were Charles Rennie Mackintosh and Alexander 'Greek' Thomson, so named because of his love of the Greek Revival style, which earned Glasgow the title City of Architecture in 1999.

Because the M8 motorway cuts through the heart of the city, the West End still has a very separate feel to the bustling centre – bohemian, stylish and a far cry from the slightly rough and run-down image of Glasgow of old. The presence of the university here also means that there's a youthful buzz to the area almost year round. While most of the sights are clustered around the city centre, the West End is the place to come to shop, drink and people-watch.

## SIGHTS & ATTRACTIONS

### Botanic Gardens
Originally intended as a private centre of learning and a place to grow

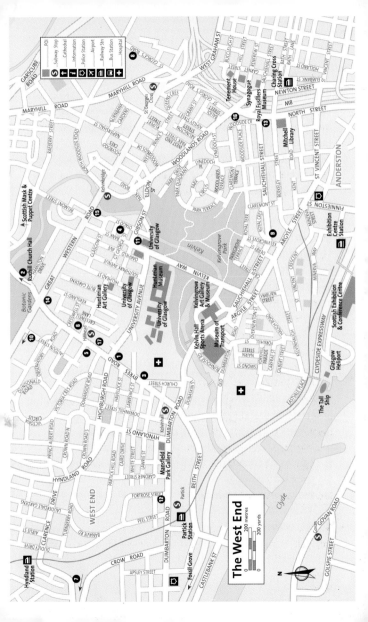

botanic specimens for the science students of Glasgow University, the beautiful botanic gardens are now very much open to the public. The highlight is the vast glasshouse with a domed ceiling. Inside are tropical plants that can only thrive in this northerly setting within these heated conditions. There's also a rose garden, a herb garden and a popular children's playing area. ⓐ Great Western Rd & Queen Margaret Drive ⓣ (0141) 276 1614 ⓦ www.glasgow.gov.uk ⓛ Gardens: 07.00–dusk; glasshouse: 10.00–18.00 Apr–Oct; 10.00–16.15 Nov–Mar ⓝ Subway: Hillhead

### Mitchell Library

This vast public reference library, open to members and non-members, contains the largest collection of works by that beloved Scottish poet Robert Burns, as well as numerous rare manuscripts, maps and documents. The library also regularly holds temporary art exhibitions. ⓐ North St ⓣ (0141) 287 2999 ⓦ www.mitchelllibrary.org ⓛ 09.00–20.00 Mon–Thur, 09.00–17.00 Fri & Sat ⓝ Suburban railway: Charing Cross

### FOSSIL GROVE

In 1887, during development of the land that is Victoria Park, 11 fossilised tree stumps were found, which indicates that a forest existed here more than 300 million years ago. The tree species, giant clubmoss, is now extinct. Today the stumps are protected in a specially constructed building but there is a viewing gallery and detailed explanations about the importance of the site. ⓐ Victoria Park ⓣ (0141) 950 1448 ⓦ www.glasgowmuseums.com ⓛ 10.00–15.30 Easter–Sept. Admission charge

○ *The Botanic Gardens are open to the public*

### Ruchill Church Hall

Yet another of Charles Rennie Mackintosh's contributions to Glasgow, this mission hall still has a regular congregation of worshippers but art lovers are equally welcome. **ⓐ** 15–17 Shakespeare St **ⓣ** (0141) 946 0466 **ⓦ** www.ruchillparish.org.uk **ⓛ** 11.00–15.00 Mon–Fri, Sept–June **Ⓝ** Subway: Kelvinbridge

## CULTURE

### Hunterian Art Gallery & Museum

After the Kelvingrove this is probably the best museum in Glasgow, originally put together from the collections of an 18th-century doctor William Hunter. Art lovers will have their fill here, with works by such masters as Rembrandt, Stubbs and Pissarro, as well as the largest collection of works by James McNeill Whistler outside the USA. There's also a significant collection of the Scottish Colourists and the art school known as the Glasgow Boys. However, the highlight of the gallery is the Mackintosh House, a reconstruction of Rennie Mackintosh's own abode on Florentine Terrace, built from plans the architect drew up himself. The museum section features displays on zoology and anatomy, as well as collections exploring prehistoric life, ancient Egypt, the Romans and the voyages of Captain Cook. **ⓐ** Gallery: Hillhead St; museum: University Avenue **ⓣ** Gallery: (0141) 330 5431; museum: (0141) 330 4221 **ⓦ** www.hunterian.gla.ac.uk **ⓛ** 09.30–17.00 Mon–Sat **Ⓝ** Subway: Hillhead. Admission charge to Mackintosh House

### Kelvingrove Art Gallery & Museum

Long the city's biggest draw for both locals and visitors, this vast Edwardian building is home to a spectacular array of art, including

🔺 *Kelvingrove Art Gallery & Museum is Glasgow's finest museum*

works by Van Gogh, Rembrandt, Botticelli and Salvador Dalí's famous *Christ of St John on the Cross*. There's also a vast weaponry collection, archaeological finds and natural history items, and a restored Spitfire suspended from the ceiling. Displays are arranged by themes within the 22 galleries. ⓐ Argyle St ⓣ (0141) 276 9599 ⓦ www.glasgowmuseums.com ⓛ 10.00–17.00 Mon–Thur & Sat, 11.00–17.00 Fri & Sun ⓝ Subway: Kelvinhall

**Museum of Transport**

The advances in transport in the 19th and 20th centuries were so extraordinary that it seems every major city these days has a museum dedicated to the subject. But this is certainly one of the best, not least because Glasgow has a long history of being at the forefront of shipbuilding, as well as railway and car manufacturing. From horse-drawn carriages to Concorde, nothing is left unexplored here, but for a real step back in time don't miss the re-created 1930s street, complete with pub, café, bakery, an underground station and cars appropriate to the time. The Clyde Room, meanwhile, explores the city's highly important contribution to shipbuilding. ❸ Bunhouse Rd, off Dumbarton Rd (opposite Kelvingrove Gallery) ❶ (0141) 287 2720 Ⓦ www.glasgowmuseums.com ❶ 10.00–17.00 Mon–Thur & Sat, 11.00–17.00 Fri & Sun Ⓝ Subway: Kelvinhall

## RETAIL THERAPY

**Coach House Trust Shop** The Coach House Trust Project endeavours to help people with mental health problems both psychologically and economically through craft workshops, and the results of their efforts are on sale here. Wooden furniture, clocks, artworks and mosaic tables are all beautifully crafted. ❸ 518 Great Western Rd ❶ (0141) 334 6888 ❶ 09.00–17.00 Mon–Sat Ⓝ Subway: Kelvinbridge

**Galletly & Tubbs** A diverse range of goods, from Italian ceramics to glass Buddhas to vegan handbags, have made this a hugely popular interior design store. ❸ 431 Great Western Rd ❶ (0141) 357 1001 ❶ 09.00–17.00 Mon–Sat, 10.00–16.00 Sun Ⓝ Subway: Kelvinbridge

**Go Potty** If you love ceramics and want to try your hand at making your own, pop in here where experienced staff can teach you the basics. ❸ 691 Great Western Rd ❶ (0141) 341 0520 ❶ 12.00–19.00 Tues–Fri, 10.00–19.00 Sat, 12.00–17.00 Sun Ⓝ Subway: Kelvinbridge

**Honey Bea's House** Adult and children's wear, designer jewellery, unusual handbags and even kitchenware are all on sale in this eclectic boutique. You could spend hours browsing here. ❸ De Courcy's Arcade, Cresswell Lane, off Cresswell St ❶ (0141) 339 0269 ❶ 10.00–17.00 Mon–Sat Ⓝ Subway: Hillhead

**Hyndland Book Shop** If you want to know more about Glasgow, and Scotland in general, this is the place of choice, stocking a wide range of titles dedicated to the subject. ⓐ 143 Hyndland Rd ⓣ (0141) 334 5522 ⓛ 09.30–18.00 Mon–Sat ⓝ Subway: Kelvinhall

**I J Mellis** A wonderful cheesemonger with international produce, as well as traditional accompaniments such as oatcakes. ⓐ 492 Great Western Rd ⓣ (0141) 339 8998 ⓦ www.mellischeese.co.uk ⓛ 09.00–18.30 Mon–Sat ⓝ Subway: Kelvinbridge

**I Love Candy** Anyone with a sweet tooth should check out this vintage sweet shop, which specialises in forgotten and discontinued classics. ⓐ 261 Byres Rd ⓣ (0141) 337 3399 ⓦ www.ilovecandystore.com ⓛ 09.00–17.00 Mon–Sat ⓝ Subway: Hillhead

**JKJ** Beautiful designer jewellery by the shop's owner, Judith Kenny. She'll also be happy to take on commissions if you want a special piece made. ⓐ 9 Park Rd ⓣ (0141) 334 0995 ⓛ 10.30–17.30 Tues & Sat ⓝ Subway: Kelvinbridge

**Pink Poodle** A wonderful array of funky fashion created by a range of young designers. ⓐ 181 Byres Rd ⓣ (0141) 357 3344 ⓛ 09.00–18.00 Mon–Sat ⓝ Subway: Hillhead

**The Studio** The West End is the best area in Glasgow for antique hunting, and The Studio is a treasure trove of genuine, well-sourced antiques. A speciality here are the art nouveau tiles, but there's also all manner of furniture, lamp shades, fire grates and books. ⓐ De Courcy's Arcade, Cresswell Lane, off Cresswell St ⓣ (0141) 334 8211 ⓛ 10.00–17.30 Tues–Sat, 10.00–17.00 Sun

## TAKING A BREAK

**Little Italy £ ❶** Part deli, part café, you can buy delicious slices of pizza to go. ⓐ 205 Byres Rd ❶ (0141) 339 6287 ⓦ www.littleitalyglasgow.com ⓛ 12.00–00.00 ⓝ Subway: Hillhead

**North Star Provisions £ ❷** Iain Mackenzie's ever-popular deli and café serves breakfasts all day, tortillas and other wraps, freshly squeezed juices and great coffee. ⓐ 108 Queen Margaret Dr ❶ (0141) 946 5365 ⓛ 08.00–18.00 Mon, 08.00–19.00 Tues–Thur, 08.00–20.00 Fri & Sat, 11.00–18.00 Sun

**University Café £ ❸** This has been a West End institution since 1918 and is, as its name would suggest, very popular with students. Its ice cream is legendary. ⓐ 87 Byres Rd ❶ (0141) 339 5217 ⓛ 09.00–22.00 Mon–Sat, 10.00–22.00 Sun ⓝ Subway: Kelvinhall

**Tattie Mac's ££ ❹** A comfortable bistro-style place that is equally good for coffee or a full lunchtime meal. ⓐ 61 Otago St, Hillhead ❶ (0141) 337 2282 ⓛ 11.00–22.00 ⓝ Subway: Kelvinbridge

## AFTER DARK

**The Bothy £ ❺** Scottish food at its hearty best – no frills here, just good honest cooking and delicious at that. ⓐ 11 Ruthven Lane (off Saltoun St) ❶ (0141) 334 4040 ⓛ 12.00–14.30, 17.30–22.00 Mon–Sat ⓝ Subway: Hillhead

**Café Andaluz £ ❻** A wonderful Spanish tapas restaurant decorated in the Moorish style typical of Andalucia. Try fried chorizo sausage in wine or spicy prawns or, for a larger meal, the traditional Spanish paella. A great place to go with a group of friends, when you can mix and match all the different dishes. ❷ 2 Cresswell Lane, off Cresswell St ❶ (0141) 339 1111 ❿ www.cafeandaluz.com ⏱ 12.00–23.00 Mon–Sat, 12.30–22.30 Sun Ⓝ Subway: Hillhead

**Café Royale** £ ❼ Traditional Scottish fish and seafood, much of it sourced from the Argyll coast where the owners also have a hotel and restaurant. You can't get fresher than that, and it's great value too. ❷ 340 Crow Rd ❶ (0141) 338 6606 ⏱ 12.00–23.00 Mon–Sat, 12.30–22.30 Sun

**Grassroots** £ ❽ The best place in Glasgow for vegetarians – international dishes and salads that even carnivores wouldn't turn down, all served with flair. ❷ 97 St George's Rd ❶ (0141) 333 0534 ❿ www.grassrootsorganic.com ⏱ 10.00–20.45 Mon–Thur, 10.00–21.45 Fri, 10.00–15.30, 17.00–21.45 Sat, 10.00–15.30, 17.00–20.45 Sun Ⓝ Subway: St George's Cross

**Mother India** £ ❾ One of Glasgow's best-known and best-loved Indian restaurants – you should book ahead. Good choice for vegetarians. There's a small wine list but you're also welcome to bring your own. ❷ 28 Westminster Terrace, off Sauchiehall St ❶ (0141) 221 1633 ❿ www.motherindiaglasgow.co.uk ⏱ 17.30–22.30 Mon–Thur, 17.30–23.00 Fri, 13.00–23.00 Sat, 13.00–22.00 Sun

**Stazione** £ ❿ Housed in a former station ticket hall, yet despite its Italian name the main influence on the menu here is Middle Eastern cooking such as kebabs (on skewers, not in bread) and *meze*. ❷ 1051 Great Western Rd ❶ (0141) 576 7576 ⏱ 17.30–21.30

**Stravaigin £** **⑪** From Oriental-style duck to a traditional plate of haggis, neeps and tatties (swede and mashed potato), Stravaigin caters to all tastes. Its emphasis is on the freshest and most seasonal produce – one of the reasons it's become a West End institution. ⓐ 28 Gibson St ⓣ (0141) 334 2665 ⓦ www.stravaigin.com ⓛ 11.00–23.00

**Two Fat Ladies £** **⑫** If you're a fish lover you can't do much better than this. The restaurant has an excellent reputation of simply prepared fish and seafood, most of it locally sourced in Scotland, such as Loch Etive mussels. ⓐ 88 Dumbarton Rd ⓣ (0141) 339 1944 ⓦ www.twofatladiesrestaurant.com ⓛ 12.00–15.00, 17.30–22.30 ⓝ Subway: Kelvinbridge

**Loon Fung ££** **⑬** If it's popular with the local Chinese community, then you know the food is good, and Loon Fung is always buzzing. The dim sum is excellent. ⓐ 417 Sauchiehall St ⓣ (0141) 332 1240 ⓛ 11.30–04.00

**Òran Mor ££** **⑭** A lively place celebrating all that is great about Scottish culture, from food to music to whisky. ⓐ Corner of Great Western Rd & Byres Rd ⓣ (0141) 357 6200 ⓦ www.oran-mor.co.uk ⓛ Mon–Wed 09.00–02.00, Thur–Sat 09.00–03.00, Sun 12.30–03.00 ⓝ Subway: Hillhead

**La Parmigiana ££** **⑮** Considered one of the best Italian restaurants in the country, which is quite a feat considering how many Italian restaurants there are in Glasgow. Seafood and game are the best options here, such as lobster ravioli. ⓐ 447 Great Western Rd ⓣ (0141) 334 0686 ⓦ www.laparmigiana.co.uk ⓛ 12.00–14.30, 17.30–22.30 Mon–Sat

**Thai Fountain ££** ⑯ One of Glasgow's most popular Thai restaurants. As well as standards such as green curry, there are also specialities such as Volcano Chicken (chicken with Thai liqueur) and Pep Makham (duck in tamarind sauce). ⓐ 2 Woodside Crescent ⓣ (0141) 332 1599 ⓦ www.thai-fountain.com ⓛ 12.00–14.00, 17.30–23.00 Mon–Fri, 12.00–23.30 Sat ⓝ Subway: St George's Cross

**The Ubiquitous Chip £££** ⑰ Not only Glasgow's best-known restaurant, but one of the best known in Scotland. Traditional Scottish fare might include Perthshire pigeon or Ayrshire lamb. ⓐ 12 Ashton Lane, off Byres Rd ⓣ (0141) 334 5007 ⓦ www.ubiquitouschip.co.uk ⓛ 12.00–14.30, 17.30–23.00 Mon–Sat, 12.30–15.00, 18.30–23.00 Sun ⓝ Subway: Hillhead

△ *The piping lion of Òran Mor on a wall in this lively entertainment venue*

# Southside & River Clyde

For some 200 years Glasgow's Southside and the River Clyde were associated with shipbuilding and dockers and, like all port areas, had a rather shady atmosphere and reputation. When the shipbuilding stopped the area went into decline but, like so many dockland areas the world over that also witnessed a demise, the area has begun to see a regeneration in recent years. The opening of the Burrell Collection in 1983 brought visitors flocking over the river for the first time, and the area has barely looked back since. Having overcome the shock that accompanied the end of the shipping industry, the city is now keen to celebrate what it once was and there are museums dedicated solely to the subject. Meanwhile, taking advantage of cheaper rents than the West End, trendy shops, bars and restaurants have begun to move south, bringing a new injection of style to the area. Southsiders can, once again, be proud of their region.

## SIGHTS & ATTRACTIONS

### Bellahouston Park
One of Glasgow's many parks that emerged in the 19th century, created by city planners to counteract what would otherwise be an unstinting urban environment. The main feature of the park today, aside from the House for an Art Lover (see page 98), is its sporting facilities, including an 18-hole pitch and putt golf course and sports arena. ➌ Dumbreck Rd ➊ (0141) 427 0558 ⓦ www.glasgow.gov.uk ⓛ Dawn–dusk

### Celtic FC Visitor Centre & Museum
Football is the life blood of Glasgow, and anyone interested in the

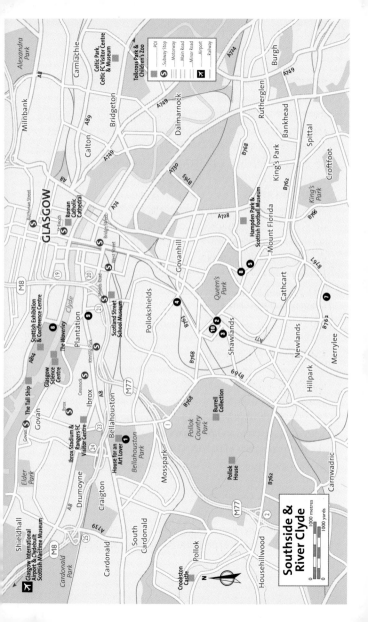

# Southside & River Clyde

**Legend**
- **S** POI
- Subway Stop
- Motorway
- Main Road
- Minor Road
- ✈ Airport
- Railway

0 1000 metres
0 1000 yards

N

Glasgow International Airport & Clydebuilt Scottish Maritime Museum

The Tall Ship

Glasgow Science Centre

Ibrox Stadium & Rangers FC Visitor Centre

House for an Art Lover

Scottish Exhibition & Conference Centre

The Waverley

Scotland Street School Museum

Burrell Collection

Pollok House

Crookston Castle

Roman Catholic Cathedral

Celtic Park, Celtic FC Visitor Centre & Museum

Tollcross Park & Children's Zoo

Hampden Park & Scottish Football Museum

**GLASGOW**

Pollok Country Park

Bellahouston Park

Queen's Park

Alexandra Park

native Celtic club should pay a visit here. The museum charts the triumphs and disappointments that are all part of the 'beautiful game' with displays of trophies and past teams, and there's also the chance to tour the stadium. ⓐ Celtic Park ⓣ (0141) 551 4308 ⓦ www.celticfc.net ⓛ Non match-day tours: 11.00, 12.00, 13.45, 14.30; Sat match-day tours: 09.30, 10.00, 10.30, 11.00. Admission charge

### Crookston Castle

This part-ruined castle dates from the 14th century but fell into decline in the 15th century. Only one of its original four towers still survives, but it's all the more evocative for that. ⓐ Brockburn Rd ⓣ (0141) 883 9606 ⓦ www.historic-scotland.gov.uk ⓛ 09.30–16.30 Apr–Sept; 09.30–16.30 Mon–Sat, 14.00–16.30 Sun, Oct–Mar

### Glasgow Science Centre

Unlike London's disastrous Millennium Dome and wobbly Millennium Bridge, Scotland's year 2000 projects were a success from the outset. The Glasgow Science Centre's gleaming structure of glass and steel is one of the best, with three floors of interactive exhibits exploring all manner of scientific advances, as well as a planetarium and an IMAX cinema. Its most popular feature, however, is its 127 m (416 ft) tower, which rotates 360 degrees. Weather permitting, visitors can take a glass lift to the top to see one of the best panoramas of the city. ⓐ Pacific Quay ⓣ (0141) 420 5000 ⓦ www.gsc.org.uk ⓛ 10.00–18.00. Admission charge

### Pollok House & Country Park

This graceful Georgian house and its surrounding park was home to the Maxwell family from 1750 until they donated it to the city in 1966. The exterior of the house is fronted by an impressive

SOUTHSIDE & RIVER CLYDE

double staircase, while inside, past the marble hallway, there are artworks by the likes of Goya, William Blake and El Greco as well as countless pieces of antique furniture and ceramics. The servants' quarters are a wonderful insight into the running of the house in days gone by. Try to visit at the weekend when costumed staff bring this aspect to life. The café is set in the original kitchen, complete with a cast-iron range. As well as containing the Burrell Collection (see page 97), the park is dotted with walking trails, some of which can be undertaken accompanied by guides.

ⓐ 2060 Pollokshaws Rd ⓣ (0141) 616 6410 ⓦ www.nts.org.uk
ⓛ House: 10.00–17.00; park: 24 hrs ⓝ Bus: 45, 47, 48, 57. Admission charge for house

### Rangers Football Club & Visitor Centre
Similar to the Celtic Football Club (see page 90), Rangers delights its fans by organising tours of its Ibrox Stadium, including the players' dressing room and the press room. An exhibition gives a full history

● *The Scottish Exhibition & Conference Centre is nicknamed the 'Armadillo'*

of the team and its numerous trophies are on display for all to see.
ⓐ Ibrox Stadium, Edmiston Drive ⓣ 0871 702 1972 ⓦ www.rangers.co.uk
ⓛ Tours: Fri–Sun, non-match days only (telephone for times)
ⓝ Subway: Ibrox. Admission charge

### Scottish Exhibition & Conference Centre (SECC)

A packed annual calendar of events is held at the SECC, the largest
exhibition centre in the city and a striking piece of silver architecture
on the Clyde, nicknamed the 'Armadillo'. Big-name rock and pop
stars stage concerts here, while exhibition areas host large-scale
events such as the Ideal Home Show. ⓐ Exhibition Way, Finnieston
ⓣ (0141) 248 3000 ⓦ www.secc.co.uk ⓛ Variable according to event,
so check website

### Seaforce boat tours

A great way to see Glasgow is from the water. Excursions range
from the whiteknuckle Clyde Ride, which gives a view of the city
from the river in a mere half an hour, or the four-hour-long Estuary
Tour, which passes through the region's sea lochs. ⓐ Boats leave from
The Tall Ship at the SECC ⓣ (0141) 221 1070 ⓦ www.seaforce.co.uk.
Admission charge

### The Tall Ship

Sadly, only five ships built on the Clyde in the long history of Glasgow's
shipbuilding industry are still afloat, and this 1896 sample, the Glenlee,
is one of them. A fuller account of the industry can be found at the
Clydebuilt Scottish Maritime Museum (see page 98), but this is a far
more evocative way to find out what life was like aboard ship and
uncover the history of a single vessel. Audio displays reproduce the
sounds of sailors' voices, clinking chains and hauling ropes, the galley

○ Find out what life was like on board an original Tall Ship

kitchen reveals the sparse and unappetising meals that were served, while the cargo hold reveals details of what was imported and exported on the often long journeys. ⓐ Glasgow Harbour, Stobcross Rd ⓘ (0141) 222 2513 ⓦ www.thetallship.com ⓛ 10.00–17.00 Mar–Oct; 10.00–16.00 Nov–Feb. Admission charge

## The Waverley

For decades the great Glaswegian annual tradition was to take a boat trip 'doon the watter' for a holiday, usually to the nearby islands of Bute and Arran. The Waverley paddlesteamer is a remnant of those days, and today visitors can take day or half-day cruises down the Firth of Clyde. ⓐ Departures from Andersons Quay ⓘ 0845 130 4647 ⓦ www.waverleyexcursions.co.uk ⓛ Apr–Oct. Admission charge

## CULTURE

## Burrell Collection

Like so many other 19th- and early 20th-century wealthy industrialists, shipping heir Sir William Burrell used his vast fortune to indulge his passion for art, eventually amassing more than 9,000 pieces from all over the world – including China and Egypt. European masters featured in the collection include Rembrandt and the famous *The Thinker* sculpture by Auguste Rodin. Burrell donated his collection to the city in 1944, but it wasn't until 1983 that the full works were opened to the public – not least because Burrell had stipulated that a gallery should be sited away from the pollution of the city centre. Pollok Park (see page 92) was donated to the city in the 1960s and

◀ *An old paddlesteamer, The Waverley, offers cruises down the Firth of Clyde*

finally provided the perfect setting to meet the collector's demands. Today the Burrell Collection is one of the most respected and popular art galleries in Britain. ⓐ Pollok Country Park, Pollokshaws Rd ⓣ (0141) 287 2550 ⓦ www.glasgowmuseums.com ⓛ 10.00–17.00 Mon–Thur & Sat, 11.00–17.00 Fri & Sun ⓥ Bus: 45, 47, 48, 57

**Clydebuilt Scottish Maritime Museum**

Shipbuilding on the Clyde was one of the greatest mainstays of the Glasgow economy – some of the world's greatest liners, including the *QE2*, were built here – until its final decline in the 1970s due to advances in transport and lack of demand. However, many still feel that it is an essential part of the Glasgow 'story', and this museum dedicates itself to the subject. With the aid of audiovisual displays, visitors are taken through the whole history from the 18th to the 20th century, and are able to witness every stage in the process of building a ship, from first nail to inaugural launch. There's also much information about the importing of tobacco that made Glasgow rich, and later the trade in cotton – both benefits from possession of the New World in the 18th century. Kids in particular will also love the interactive exhibits that allow them to 'navigate' a ship and become a trader for a day. The shop sells a variety of ship-related memorabilia. ⓐ Braehead ⓣ (0141) 886 1013 ⓦ www.scottishmaritimemuseum.org ⓛ 10.00–17.30 Mon–Sat, 11.00–17.00 Sun ⓥ Bus: 54C, 147, 398, 747 to Braehead Shopping Centre. Admission charge

**House for an Art Lover**

With plenty of original Charles Rennie Mackintosh buildings to see in the city, this reconstruction may seem a little unnecessary, but nevertheless it gives another fascinating insight into the architect

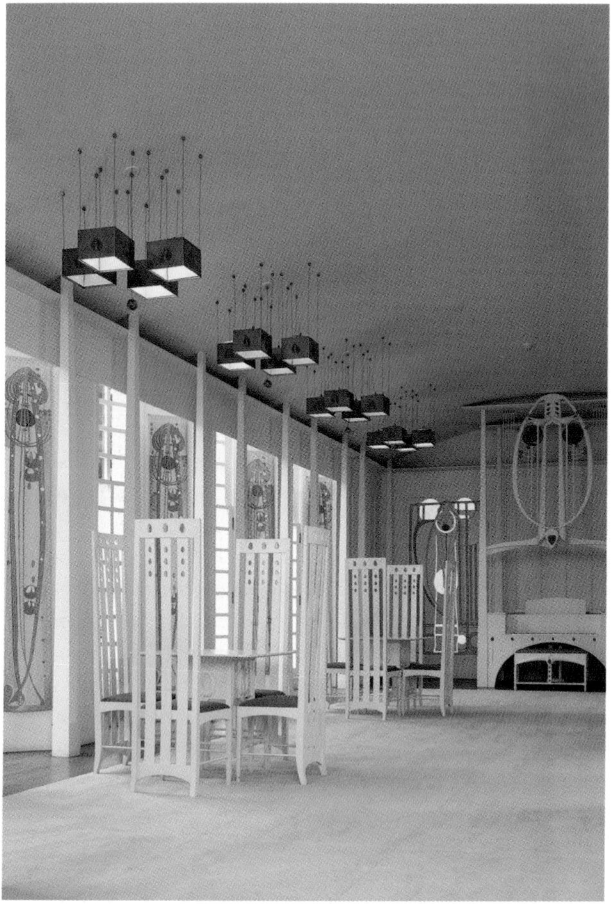

*The music room in the House for an Art Lover*

### SCOTTISH FOOTBALL MUSEUM

Celtic and Rangers may have museums devoted entirely to their own teams but, here at Hampden Park Stadium, the country's national football arena, the full history of football throughout Scotland can be explored. There are 14 different themed exhibits, uncovering the history of the sport from its earliest days to modern times, as well as an international roll of honour and a Scottish Football Hall of Fame. A tour of the stadium includes visits to the dressing room, a chance to walk through the players' tunnel, visits to the presentation area and the Royal Box and even better, for fans young and old, the chance to kick a goal in the warm-up area. ❸ Hampden Park Football Ground, Aikenhead Rd ❶ (0141) 616 6139 ❿ www.scottishfootballmuseum.org.uk ❻ 10.00–17.00 Mon–Sat, 11.00–17.00 Sun (except match days). Admission charge

and designer's visions. Built in the 1990s, it used plans and sketches drawn up by Mackintosh himself in 1901 for a house he intended to build as part of a design competition, from which he was disqualified because he submitted his work too late. The re-created rooms also display the original illustrations so visitors can compare and contrast art versus life. For anyone fond of Mackintosh's designs, the gift-shop is a treasure trove of gifts and jewellery using his trademark motifs. ❸ Bellahouston Park, 10 Dumbreck Rd ❶ (0141) 353 4770 ❿ www.houseforanartlover.co.uk ❻ 10.00–16.00 Mon–Wed, 10.00–13.00 Thur–Sun, Apr–Sept; 10.00–13.00 Sat & Sun, Oct–Mar. Admission charge

**Scotland Street School Museum**

The appeal here is two-fold: the architectural design of Rennie Mackintosh in this turn-of-the-century building; and the excellent internal exhibition detailing the history of 500 years of schooling in the city. The exhibits tell the story of education from the 15th century onwards, but it is the re-creation of 19th- and early 20th-century classrooms and playgrounds that provides the most fascinating part of the museum and reveals how rapidly teaching methods, uniforms and discipline have changed within those hundred years. ⓐ 225 Scotland St ⓣ (0141) 287 0500 ⓦ www.glasgowmuseums.com ◷ 10.00–17.00 Mon–Thur & Sat, 11.00–17.00 Fri & Sun ⓢ Subway: Shields Road

## RETAIL THERAPY

**Braehead Shopping Centre** Near the Clydebuilt Maritime Museum, this shopping centre has more than a hundred outlets of the usual chains such as Gap and Next, as well as an ice-skating rink and children's play area. ⓐ Kings Inch Rd ⓣ (0141) 885 1441 ⓦ www.braehead.co.uk ◷ 10.00–21.00 Mon–Fri, 09.00–18.30 Sat, 10.00–18.00 Sun ⓢ Bus: 54C, 147, 398, 747

**The Candle Store** All manner of candles, from the thick white church types to scented varieties, have been produced here since 1897. There's also a factory seconds area and tours to see the process of candle-making in action. ⓐ 23 Robert St ⓣ (0141) 425 1661 ⓦ www.the-candle-store.co.uk ◷ 09.00–17.00 Mon–Fri, 10.00–16.00 Sat ⓢ Subway: Govan

**Glasgow Sweet Centre** Specialists in all types of Indian and Pakistani sweets, this shop gives a taste of Asia in the heart of Glasgow. ⓐ 202 Allison St ⓣ (0141) 424 0000 ⓛ 10.00–18.00 Mon–Sat

**Silverburn** A shopping complex housing around a hundred shops, dozens of eateries, coffee shops and garden spaces. ⓐ Barrhead Rd ⓣ (0141) 880 3200 ⓦ www.silverburn.com ⓛ 10.00–21.00 Mon–Fri, 09.00–19.00 Sat, 10.00–18.00 Sun ⓝ Bus: X8, X8A

## TAKING A BREAK

**Art Lovers' Café £ ❶** As part of the House for an Art Lover (see page 98), this bright and airy café is a wonderful lunch or tea stop, decorated with a changing display of works by Scottish artists. ⓐ Bellahouston Park, 10 Dumbreck Rd ⓣ (0141) 353 4779 ⓦ www.houseforanartlover.co.uk ⓛ 10.00–17.00; lunch: 12.00–16.00

**Brooklyn Café £ ❷** Pasta, pizza, salads and delicious desserts are perfect for a quite substantial lunch. ⓐ 21 Minard Rd ⓣ (0141) 632 3427 ⓛ 08.00–19.00 Mon–Sat, 09.00–19.00 Sun

**Jam £ ❸** One of the cafés and restaurants that is helping to turn Southside into the city's hotspot. Decorated in retro style, coffee and sandwiches are served all day. ⓐ 28 Kilmarnock Rd ⓣ 0845 659 5902 ⓛ 08.00–19.00 Mon–Sat, 09.00–19.00 Sun

**Mise en Place £ ❹** Also a restaurant in the evening, this is a lovely place for a light lunch, serving pasta, crêpes, fish cakes and more. ⓐ 122–124 Nithsdale Rd ⓣ (0141) 424 4600 ⓦ www.misenplace.co.uk ⓛ 10.00–21.00

## AFTER DARK

### RESTAURANTS

**Alishan £** ❺ Specialists in Indian and Pakistani dishes, with plenty to choose from if you're vegetarian. ⓐ 250 Battlefield Rd ❶ (0141) 632 5294 ⓦ www.alishantandoori.co.uk ❶ 17.30–22.30

**Yen £–££** ❻ A mix of all things oriental here. Upstairs is the cheaper noodle-style bar, while downstairs you can experience a traditional Japanese *teppanyaki* menu consisting of eight courses. ⓐ 28 Tunnel St ❶ (0141) 847 0110 ❶ 12.00–14.00, 17.00–23.00 Mon–Fri, 12.00–23.30 Sat, 17.00–22.30 Sun

**Ashoka Southside ££** ❼ The menu here is mostly influenced by the subcontinent from Persia to Pakistan and India, although haggis has been known to pop up on the menu from time to time. ⓐ 268 Clarkston Rd ❶ (0141) 637 0711 ❶ 17.00–23.30 Sun–Thur, 17.00–00.00 Fri & Sat

**Battlefield Rest ££** ❽ A popular Italian restaurant with a particularly fine seafood menu and a wonderful range of homemade breads. ⓐ 55 Battlefield Rd ❶ (0141) 636 6955 ⓦ www.battlefieldrest.co.uk ❶ 10.00–22.00 Mon–Sat

**La Fiorentina ££** ❾ Specialising in Tuscan cuisine and with a wine list of more than 150 choices, this is one of the area's most popular Italian offerings. Try the delicious trio of monkfish, lobster and king prawns. ⓐ 2 Paisley Rd West ❶ (0141) 420 1585 ⓦ www.la-fiorentina.com ❶ 12.00–14.15, 17.30–22.30 Mon–Sat ⓝ Subway: Shields Road

**Tusk ££ 🔟** Set in a converted cinema and decorated with a 10 m (30 ft) Buddha statue, huge draping curtains and a long mahogany bar. The menu has an Oriental influence, such as beef teriyaki, but there are also staple favourites such as fish and chips. One of the most stylish places on the Southside. 🟢 18 Moss-Side Rd 🟠 (0141) 649 9199 🕐 17.00–22.30 Thur–Sun

## PUBS & BARS

**The Bank** A local bar and bistro, this former bank has a stylish interior far removed from its ageing architecture and has a good menu with reasonable prices. 🟢 443 Clarkston Rd 🟠 (0141) 637 8461 🕐 11.00–00.00

**Clutha Vaults** A dark Victorian pub, complete with snugs. Live music at the weekends. 🟢 167 Stockwell St 🟠 (0141) 552 7520 🕐 11.00–23.30

**The Old Toll Bar** Lovely Victorian pub decorated with a marble bar, leather seats and opulent mirrors. There's also a restaurant downstairs. 🟢 1–3 Paisley Rd West 🟠 (0141) 429 3135 🕐 10.30–14.30, 17.30–23.00

**Scotia Bar** Tudor-beamed pub, popular with poets and folk and blues musicians. Claims to be the city's oldest pub, although this isn't proven. 🟢 112 Stockwell St 🟠 (0141) 552 8681 🗑 www.scotiabar.net 🕐 10.30–23.30

---

▶ *Balloch Castle is set in a country park at the southern end of Loch Lomond*

OUT OF TOWN
trips

# Clyde Valley

Rising in the border hills south of the city, the River Clyde flows through Glasgow and the heartland of industrial Scotland on its way to the Irish Sea. Along its banks are industrial and rural heritage sites, medieval castles, modern purpose-built visitor attractions, and some of southern Scotland's most attractive scenery, with landscaped parks, waterfalls and wooded glens where peregrine falcons nest. One of Scotland's busiest highways, the M74 motorway, passes through the region en route to Carlisle and northern England, yet surprisingly few visitors detour from the main road to explore the rich hinterland of the Clyde Valley. Despite its coal-mining and iron-smelting past, the region is full of opportunities to get away from the buzz of the city. There are a plethora of country parks and wildlife reserves offering gentle strolls or longer walks, and it's always a pleasure to see the River Clyde and its tributary streams and rivers.

## GETTING THERE

There are trains from Glasgow Central (see page 48) to East Kilbride, Hamilton, Motherwell, Lanark and Paisley. Buses travel from St Enoch Centre, Glasgow to all points in Lanarkshire and Renfrewshire.

## SIGHTS & ATTRACTIONS

### Amazonia

Just outside Motherwell (off junction 5 of the M74 motorway), Amazonia is one of Scotland's biggest indoor attractions, with exotic plants and animals – including scorpions, bats, snakes, lizards and cute marmosets – in an artificial rainforest environment.

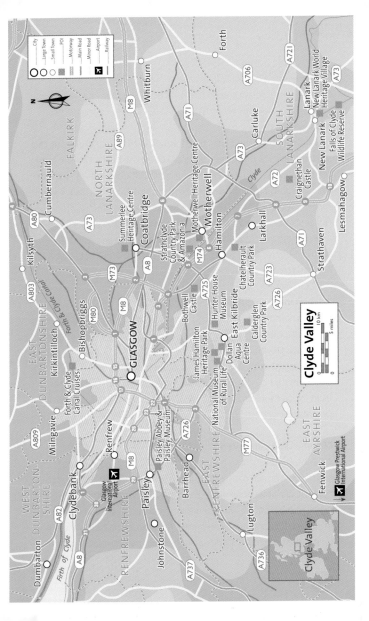

OUT OF TOWN

🄰 Strathclyde Country Park, Motherwell 🄣 (01698) 333777
🅆 www.ama-zone-ia.com 🄬 10.00–18.00. Admission charge

## Bothwell Castle

Overlooking the River Clyde, this dramatic 13th-century ruin was the
seat of the Black Douglases, allies of Robert the Bruce, and the most
powerful dynasty in these parts during the Middle Ages. It is one of
the largest and most striking of Scotland's early castles and is a real
slice of brooding, atmospheric history just a few kilometres from the
city centre. 🄰 Castle Avenue, 24 km (15 miles) southeast of Glasgow
at Uddingston, off the B7071 🄣 (01698) 616894 🅆 www.historic-
scotland.gov.uk 🄬 09.30–17.30 Apr–Sept; 09.30–16.30 Oct–Mar.
Admission charge

## Calderglen Country Park

Here you can take country walks along the River Calder and its
waterfalls. The park also has a visitor centre, children's zoo and an
adventure playground. 🄰 South of East Kilbride on A726 🄣 Visitor
centre: (01355) 236644 🄬 Park: 24 hrs; conservatory & zoo: 10.00–20.30
May–Sept, 10.00–16.30 Oct–Mar, 10.00–19.30 Apr; visitor centre:
10.30–17.00 Mon–Fri, 10.30–17.30 Sat & Sun, Apr–Sept; 11.00–16.00
Oct–Mar

## Chatelherault Country Park

This outstanding grand hunting lodge and its walled gardens
are all that remain of one of Scotland's greatest aristocratic estates,
the seat of the wealthy and powerful dukes of Hamilton. An even
grander ducal palace was abandoned and demolished in the 1920s
after extensive mining undermined its foundations, but this graceful
pink sandstone building, designed by William Adam and built in

◢ *The formal garden at Chatelherault*

1732, survived and was restored during the 1980s. It is surrounded by vast grounds where white cattle roam and centuries-old oak trees – some more than 500 years old – flourish. The River Avon flows through the grounds, and there are several guided walks, as well as a visitor centre that illustrates the history and natural heritage of the estate. ❸ Ferniegair, 2½ km (1½ miles) southeast of Hamilton on A72 ❶ (01698) 426213 ❺ House: 10.00–16.30 Mon–Thur, 12.00–16.30 Sun; visitor centre: 10.00–17.00 Mon–Sat, 12.00–17.00 Sun

## Craignethan Castle

Built in 1530 by Sir James Hamilton of Finnart, Craignethan is a rare example of a castle purpose built to withstand bombardment by cannon, with a vaulted stone caponier (bunker), a sturdy residential tower and landscaped gardens. ❸ Off the A72, 1 km (half a mile) north of Crossford village ❶ (01555) 860364 ❿ www.historic-

### STRATHCLYDE COUNTRY PARK

With 405 ha (1,000 acres) of park and woodland surrounding a man-made lake, Strathclyde Country Park is Scotland's most popular open-air activity centre, offering sailing, boating, canoeing, parascending and cycling. It even has its own beach. Equipment can be hired for all activities. Within the park is **M & D's**, Scotland's biggest theme park (❶ (01698) 333777 ❿ www.scotlandsthemepark.co.uk). ❸ Midway between Motherwell and Hamilton, off M74 (junction 5), 16 km (10 miles) south of Glasgow ❺ Park: dawn–dusk; water sports centre: 08.00–20.00. Admission charge for water sports centre & theme park

scotland.gov.uk ⏲ 09.30–17.30 Apr–Sept; 09.30–16.30 Oct;
09.30–16.30 Sat & Sun, Nov–Mar. Admission charge

### Dollan Aqua Centre

In the centre of East Kilbride, this wet and wild leisure centre has
a huge 50 m (164 ft) pool with water slides and play area. ⓐ Town
Centre Park, East Kilbride ☎ (01355) 260000 ⏲ 07.30–22.00 Mon–Fri,
08.00–17.00 Sat & Sun. Admission charge

### Falls of Clyde Wildlife Reserve

The Clyde, which powered New Lanark's mills, flows through the
village. Upstream is the Scottish Wildlife Trust's Falls of Clyde Wildlife
Reserve, with several kilometres of well-kept paths along the river
and through wooded gorges where rare peregrine falcons nest in
spring and early summer. There is a hide from which you can watch
the peregrines' nests without disturbing the adult birds or their
chicks. The river also attracts kingfishers, buzzards, dippers and
other birds, as well as otter and deer. ⓐ Scottish Wildlife Trust
Visitor Centre, New Lanark ☎ (01555) 665262 ⏲ 11.00–17.00
Mar–Dec; 12.00–16.00 Jan & Feb. Admission charge

### Forth & Clyde Canal Cruises

Narrowboat day trips on the Forth & Clyde Canal, which was built
in 1790 and is gradually being restored, make for a pleasant day out.
ⓐ Forth & Clyde Canal Society, Bishopbriggs, Glasgow ☎ (0141) 772 1620
⏲ Variable, so phone to check

### James Hamilton Heritage Park

This country park on the outskirts of East Kilbride has a sailing
loch with dinghies and sailboards for hire, as well as pedaloes,

○ *Inside Paisley Abbey*

kayaks, canoes and rowing boats. ⓐ Stewartfield Way, East Kilbride
ⓘ (01355) 276611 ⓛ Dawn–dusk, Apr–Oct

## Paisley Abbey

The former weaving town of Paisley, just south of Glasgow International
Airport, is now a residential suburb of Glasgow, with a handful of sights
of its own. Most important is Paisley Abbey, with its medieval carvings,
14th–15th-century nave and colourful stained glass. King Robert III's
tomb is in the choir, and the abbey also contains the ancient Barochan
Cross, dating from the dawn of Celtic Christianity. Founded in 1163 by
Cluniac monks, the church was partly destroyed during the Reformation
and was restored during the 19th century. ⓐ Abbey Close, Paisley
ⓘ (0141) 889 7654 ⓛ 10.00–15.30 Mon–Sat, Services 11.00, 12.15 & 18.30 Sun

## CULTURE

### Hunter House Museum

Also in East Kilbride is the Hunter House Museum, the birthplace
of two luminaries of 18th-century Scotland, the brothers John and
William Hunter. An interactive exhibition describes their achievements
in medicine and science. ⓐ Maxwelltown Rd, East Kilbride
ⓘ (01355) 261261 ⓛ 12.30–16.30 Mon–Fri, 12.00–17.00 Sat & Sun,
Apr–Sept

### Motherwell Heritage Centre

An important centre of the iron and steel industry until the 1950s,
Motherwell has begun to reinvent itself as a centre of excellence
for the knowledge economy – but in many ways it's little more than
a suburb. Its chief attraction is the stunning Motherwell Heritage
Centre. This remarkable, space-age building opened in 1996 and is

one of Scotland's most striking modern museums, with a viewing platform that offers sweeping views of the valley of the River Clyde. The Technopolis interactive display follows the area's history from the days of the Roman legions, through the 19th-century heyday of the Age of Steam, to the present day. There's also an excellent foyer gallery with a changing programme of exhibitions. **ⓐ** 1 High Rd, Motherwell **ⓣ** (01698) 251000 **ⓛ** 10.00–17.00 Thur, 10.00–19.00 Wed, Fri & Sat, 12.00–17.00 Sun

### National Museum of Rural Life

East Kilbride, where this museum is located, is a functional, purpose built 'new town' on Glasgow's southern outskirts, created during the 1960s. The museum, an annex of the National Museum of Scotland in Edinburgh, was built around a working farm and there is a collection of buildings, animals and farming equipment that show how the land was farmed during the first half of the 20th century. The farm and its Georgian farmhouse were the property of generations of the Reid family since the 16th century, and were donated to the National Trust for Scotland in 1992. The museum also has a year-round calendar of events, ranging from classic car and heavy horse shows to country fairs and collectors' events. **ⓐ** Wester Kittochside, Philipshill Rd (off Stewartfield Way), East Kilbride **ⓣ** (0131) 247 4368 **ⓦ** www.nms.ac.uk **ⓛ** 10.00–17.00. Admission charge

### New Lanark World Heritage Village

This impressive beacon of enlightened capitalism was built in the late 18th century and founded by a Scottish industrialist, David Dale (1739–1806). Under the management of Dale's son-in-law, Robert Owen (1771–1858), the water-powered cotton mills employed more than

2,000 workers. They were given decent housing, fair wages, free health care, training and schooling – including the world's first nursery school – within the first ever properly planned industrial community. Although the last weaving mills closed in 1962, New Lanark has been restored and preserved as a living community with an award-winning visitor centre, working cotton-weaving machinery, and interactive displays that tell the story of the community and its visionary founder. ⓐ 2km (1 mile) south of Lanark ⓣ (01555) 661345

🔺 *The Scottish Wildlife Trust's Falls of Clyde*

🔺 *Robert Owen's utopian village, New Lanark*

Ⓦ www.newlanark.org 🕐 10.30–17.00 June–Aug; 11.00–17.00
Sept–May. Admission charge

### Paisley Museum

Paisley is also famous as the home of the colourful 'Paisley shawls',
woven from fine wool in patterns copied from the traditional styles
of northern India. Many of these beautiful shawls are on show in
the Paisley Museum in the town centre, which also has an excellent
collection of pottery and 19th-century Scottish landscapes and portraits.
Paisley claims to be the birthplace of the great 14th-century Scottish
patriot, William Wallace, and a 19th-century monument at Elderslie,
south of the town centre, commemorates him. 🅐 High St, Paisley
🅘 (0141) 889 3151 🕐 10.00–17.00 Tues–Sat, 14.00–17.00 Sun

## Summerlee Heritage Centre

This huge centre has undergone a £10m redevelopment. It showcases working machinery from vanished local industries, an old-fashioned tramway and a re-created coal mine with a row of typical miners' cottages, all built on the site of a 19th-century ironworks.
ⓐ Heritage Way, Coatbridge, 24 km (15 miles) east of Glasgow centre
ⓣ (01236) 638460 ⓛ 10.00–17.00 Apr–Oct; 10.00–16.00 Nov–Mar

## AFTER DARK

**Cricklewood £** Brasserie-style restaurant in a quiet suburb near Bothwell Castle. Open-air tables in summer. ⓐ 27 Hamilton Rd
ⓣ (01698) 853172 ⓛ 12.00–23.00 Mon–Wed, 12.00–00.00 Thur, 11.00–00.00 Fri & Sat, 11.00–23.00 Sun

**The Crown Tavern £** A great place to relax with a pint and a pub lunch, this bar also serves evening meals and is a popular choice.
ⓐ 17 Hope St ⓣ (01555) 664639 ⓛ 10.30–14.00, 18.30–23.00

**Lanark Steayban £** Village pub-restaurant with an above-average menu.
ⓐ Glassford, near Lanark ⓣ (01357) 523400 ⓦ www.steayban.co.uk
ⓛ 11.30–15.30, 18.30–23.00

**East India Company ££** An extremely good restaurant serving authentic Indian cuisine. ⓐ 32 Wellgate, Lanark ⓣ (01555) 663827
ⓛ 11.30–14.30, 17.30–23.00 Mon–Sat

**La Vigna ££** Great classic Italian restaurant in Lanark, handily close to New Lanark. Open lunch and dinner. Good wine list. ⓐ 40 Wellgate, Lanark ⓣ (01555) 664320 ⓦ www.lavigna.co.uk ⓛ 11.00–15.00, 18.30–23.00

# Loch Lomond & the Trossachs National Park

Glasgow's urban tentacles spread more than 16 km (10 miles) north and west of the city. But then there's a sharp change in the scenery as city streets and suburbs give way to wooded river valleys, rolling moorlands and hills, and the broad expanse of Loch Lomond, with its yachts, cruisers and dozens of tiny islands. Designated as Scotland's first national park in 2001, it covers 1,865 sq m (720 sq miles) and embraces wild open spaces in the Trossach hills, lonely medieval castles, pretty villages and gentle glens, with more than 50 rivers offering fine trout fishing. There are also more than 20 smaller lochs as well as the 'inland sea' of Loch Lomond – and it's all on Glasgow's doorstep.

This part of the world is associated with two of Scotland's most famous heroes (or anti-heroes, if you come from south of the border): William Wallace (1272–1305), Guardian of Scotland in the independence struggle of the early 14th century, and the outlaw, cattle-thief, Jacobite rebel and all-around swashbuckler Rob Roy McGregor (1671–1734). Both of these reputedly took refuge from their English pursuers in the woods and glens of the Trossachs. Wallace was, of course, eventually captured and gorily executed. Rob, on the other hand, was pardoned for his offences in 1725 and died in his bed at 63 – not a bad innings, considering his chosen career.

If Luss looks oddly familiar, that's because this designated conservation village has been used as a location for a number of film and TV productions such as the highly regarded STV series *Take the High Road*. Luss is far and away the prettiest of the lochside villages, with neat little cottages laid out along narrow streets. It was built by one of the less unpleasant local lairds as a model village for his tenants in the 19th century, and has a number of

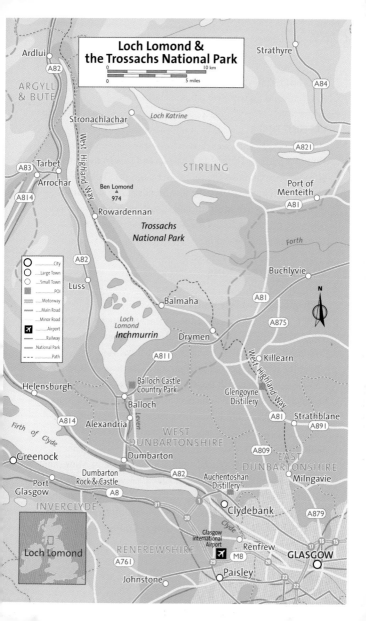

# Loch Lomond &
# the Trossachs National Park

0                    10 km

0              5 miles

Ardlui

**A82**

Strathyre

**A84**

ARGYLL
& BUTE

Stronachlachar

Loch Katrine

STIRLING

**A821**

Tarbet

**A83**

Arrochar

**A814**

Ben Lomond
▲
974

Rowardennan

Trossachs
National Park

Port of
Menteith

**A81**

Forth

Buchlyvie

**A81**

**A875**

Luss

Balmaha

Inchmurrin

Loch
Lomond

Drymen

West Highland Way

Killearn

**A811**

Glengoyne
Distillery

West Highland Way

Helensburgh

Balloch Castle
Country Park

**A81**

Strathblane

**A891**

Balloch

**A814**

Alexandria

Leven

WEST
DUNBARTONSHIRE

**A809**

EAST
DUNBARTONSHIRE

Firth of Clyde

Greenock

Dumbarton

Milngavie

Port
Glasgow

Dumbarton
Rock & Castle

**A82**

Auchentoshan
Distillery

**A8**

31

1

INVERCLYDE

30

Clydebank

Clyde

**A879**

Loch Lomond

RENFREWSHIRE

**A761**

Glasgow
International
Airport

Renfrew

**M8**

17  16  15

GLASGOW

Johnstone

Paisley

29

26

23

22

N

| | |
|---|---|
| ○ | City |
| ○ | Large Town |
| ○ | Small Town |
| □ | POI |
| ▮ | Motorway |
| | Main Road |
| | Minor Road |
| ✈ | Airport |
| | Railway |
| | National Park |
| | Path |

nice places to stay, several pleasant pubs and restaurants, and a scattering of quite stylish gift and craft shops.

## GETTING THERE

There are buses to Dumbarton, Balloch and Luss from Buchanan Bus Station in Glasgow city centre (see page 49). These are operated by First (see page 54). There are also **Scottish Citylink Coaches** (❶ 0870 550 5050) and Strathclyde Passenger Transport services (see page 56). By car, follow the M8/A82 west to Balloch via Dumbarton and Alexandria.

## SIGHTS & ATTRACTIONS

### Auchentoshan Distillery Visitor Centre

On the way to Loch Lomond (just off the A82), Auchentoshan is the closest distillery to Glasgow and is the only one in Scotland to triple-distil its malt in traditional copper pot stills. You can learn about the whole process, from malting to the final product – and sample a dram or two at the end of the tour. ❸ Dalmuir, Clydebank ❶ (01389) 878561 ❿ www.auchentoshan.co.uk ❶ Guided tours 10.00–16.00 Mon–Sat. Admission charge

### Balloch

At the southern end of Loch Lomond, Balloch is the starting point for cruises around the loch and its island. It is a popular angling, sailing and water sports centre, with several marinas, a handful of pubs and restaurants and a plethora of places to stay. For cruise timetables and tickets, contact **Sweeney's Cruises** (❶ 01389 752 376 ❿ www.sweeneyscruises.com).

## Balloch Castle Country Park

Balloch Castle Country Park, bordering the national park, was once the estate of one of medieval Scotland's most influential noble families. The small castle is more modern than it looks, dating as it does from the 19th century, and it houses a visitor centre. Balloch's 80 ha (200 acre) expanse of landscaped, wooded gardens is gradually being restored. ❶ (01389) 722600 Ⓦ www.visit-balloch.com ❶ Park: 24 hrs; visitor centre: 10.00–17.00 Easter–Oct

## Ben Lomond

Ben Lomond, 974 m (3,163 ft) above sea level, is the most prominent summit in the national park. It is an easy enough hike, with the softest route starting from Rowardennan village on the east side of the loch. Allow at least six hours for the walk to the top and back, and bring good boots and waterproof outerwear.

## Dumbarton

Dumbarton, on the north shore of the Clyde, is the gateway to Loch Lomond. Now a dormitory suburb of Glasgow, it was a famous shipbuilding centre during the 19th century and in even earlier times was the capital of two Dark Age kingdoms.

## Dumbarton Rock & Castle

Dumbarton Rock, a 76 m (250 ft) high crag, has been fortified for at least 2,000 years. In the fifth and sixth centuries AD it was the capital of the kingdom of the Britons of Strathclyde. It later became the seat of the earliest Scottish kings, who made it their capital until 1018, when they relocated to Dunfermline on the Firth of Forth. Today, the battlements and cannon of Dumbarton Castle, dating from the 18th and 19th centuries, still dominate the rock. Within

the area is a 12th-century gateway, a gloomy dungeon and a sundial presented to the keepers of the castle by Mary Queen of Scots.

ⓐ Castle Rd, Dumbarton ⓣ (01389) 732167 ⓦ www.historic-scotland.gov.uk ⓛ 09.30–16.45 Apr–Sept; 09.30–15.45 Oct–Mar. Admission charge

### Glengoyne Distillery

In the Campsie Fells (the foothills of the Trossachs), the Glengoyne Distillery has been making fine single malt whiskies since 1833. Drawing its water from a 15 m (50 ft) high waterfall nearby, Glengoyne,

● *Dumbarton Castle looks out over the Firth of Clyde*

with its whitewashed walls and slate roofs, is one of Scotland's
most picturesque distilleries. It is also one of the few that still distil
distinctive single malt whiskies in this part of the country. There are
guided tours of the still rooms and vaulted cellars, culminating in a
sampling of Glengoyne's fine malts in a stylish reception room with
views of the falls and the glen. ➋ 30 minutes from Glasgow on A81,
south of Killearn village ➊ (01360) 550254 ➍ www.glengoyne.com
➌ Tours: hourly 10.00–16.00 Mon–Sat, 12.00–16.00 Sun, Mar–Nov;
11.00–15.00 Mon–Sat, 12.00–15.00 Sun, Dec–Feb. Admission charge

### Loch Lomond & its islands

Loch Lomond is the largest body of fresh water in Britain. Roughly
triangular, the loch is some 38 km (24 miles) from north to south and
6 km (4 miles) across at its widest, reaching depths of 190 m (623 ft).
From the loch, the River Leven flows southwest to meet the Clyde at
Dumbarton. It's a lovely place to visit at any time of year, but is
undeniably at its most attractive in summer, when the still waters
of the loch reflect the greenery of birch and beech woodland all
around it. One of the finest (and most accessible) panoramic views
is from the top of aptly named Conic Hill, at Balmaha on the east
shore of the loch. It takes about 90 minutes to climb to the top,
358 m (1,164 ft) above sea level, from the Balmaha village car park.

Wildlife in the national park includes raptors such as the golden
eagle and the osprey; winter migrant waterfowl like goldeneye
ducks, whooper swans and white-fronted geese; and red and fallow
deer. The loch is dotted with around 20 islands, each with its own
picturesque history. Some are accessible if you have your own boat,
others are privately owned and off limits to visitors. The largest, and
most accessible, is Inchmurrin, where early medieval monks built
a chapel dedicated to St Mirren (*inch* is the Gaelic word for 'island',

hence Inchmurrin means 'Mirren's Island'). Since the 1930s, the island has been farmed by the Scott family, who offer summer accommodation in self-catering chalets and cottages on the farm and operate a licensed bar and restaurant for day visitors.

Other islands on the loch include Clairinch and Inch Cailloch, both of which are managed by Scottish Natural Heritage and can be visited by arrangement. Inchmoan and Inchtavannach are managed by Luss Estates, one of the biggest local landowners. Inchfad and Inchcruin are privately owned and Inchconnachan is home to more than 40 wallabies, which were introduced to the island by Lady Arran in 1980. Two smaller islands are said to have connections with two great Scottish patriots. Inchlonaig ('island of yews') is said to have been planted with yew trees to provide wood to make bows for Robert the

🔺 *Loch Lomond with snow-capped Ben Lomond*

Bruce's army – a long-term project if ever there was one, as the slow-growing yew takes decades or centuries to mature. Wallace's Island is, of course, claimed to have been one of William Wallace's hideouts – but it's rather more likely that the island simply belonged to a landowner of the same name.

**Loch Lomond & the Trossachs National Park** ☎ (01389) 722600
🌐 www.lochlomond-trossachs.org
**Loch Lomond Shores visitor centre** 📍 Ben Lomond Way, Balloch
☎ (01389) 751035 🌐 www.lochlomondshores.com 🕐 10.00–17.00
**Balmaha visitor centre** ☎ (01389) 722100
**Luss visitor centre** ☎ (01389) 722120

## LOCH LOMOND'S GREAT OUTDOORS

Loch Lomond and its surroundings provide a huge choice of outdoor activities ranging from gentle loch-side strolls to strenuous mountain hiking, long-distance walking and rock climbing; Dumbarton Rock offers one of the world's toughest technical climbs.

If you want to get on your bike, the Glasgow to Loch Lomond Cycleway (National Cycle Route Network 75) stretches 34 km (21 miles) from Glasgow city centre to Loch Lomond, then carries on all the way to Killin in Perthshire, following decommissioned railway tracks, canal towpaths, side roads and forest trails. For details contact **Sustrans** (❶ (0131) 539 8122 Ⓦ www.sustrans.org.uk) or visit Ⓦ www.cyclingscotland.com.

Loch Lomond is popular with yacht and dinghy sailors and powerboat sailors (who have objected strenuously to

## RETAIL THERAPY

**Auchentoshan Distillery Shop** For whisky lovers, this shop offers a full range of lowland single malt whiskies from the famous distillery (see page 120), as well as glassware, hip flasks and other dram-related paraphernalia. ❸ Dalmuir, Clydebank ❶ (01389) 878561 Ⓦ www.auchentoshan.co.uk ❷ Shop: 10.00–16.00; tours: Mon–Sat only. Admission charge

**Loch Lomond Shores** This large outlet shopping and leisure centre sits slightly incongruously at the south end of Loch Lomond, on

the national park's proposals to impose strict speed limits on the loch to protect wildlife). You can rent sailing boats and powerboats at several marinas at Balloch and nearby.

With 20 munros (summits over 914 m/3,000 ft), the Trossachs offer energetic hill walking on Glasgow's doorstep. Additionally, Scotland's finest long-distance walking route, the **West Highland Way** (Ⓦ www.west-highland-way.co.uk), starts in Milngavie, on the northwest outskirts of Glasgow, and passes through the national park on its way to Fort William, on the west coast. If you are planning on walking or hiking, come prepared for changeable weather at any time of year. Good boots and waterproof outerwear are essential, even in summer, and proper planning and preparation are vital for winter walks on the hills, with snow and freezing temperatures possible from October until the end of May on higher ground.

the outskirts of Balloch. Retailers include a number of Scotland's biggest names as well as international brands, a giant film screen shows the Legend of Loch Lomond presentation, and there is a children's play area. ⓐ Balloch ⓣ (01389) 751035 Ⓦ www.lochlomondshores.com ⓛ 10.00–18.00; hours may vary for individual shops

## TAKING A BREAK

**La Scarpetta £** Good, simple and inexpensive southern Italian cooking. ⓐ Balloch Rd, Balloch ⓣ (01389) 758247 ⓛ 12.00–23.00

🔺 *The large shopping and leisure centre of Loch Lomond Shores*

**The Cruin Bar & Restaurant** **££** A great local restaurant with a seafood-dominated menu and views north to Ben Lomond and across the loch to Inchmurrin Island. ❸ Loch Lomond Castle Lodges, Arden ❶ (01389) 850588 ⓦ www.thecruin.com ❶ 12.00–14.30, 17.00–21.00 Mon–Fri, 12.00–21.00 Sat & Sun

**Windows on the Loch** **££** The restaurant of the Duck Bay Hotel is well named, with great views of the loch and Ben Lomond, a classic à la carte menu and a casual dining area. The wine list is extensive

and features Old and New World wines. ❷ Arden, by Balloch
❶ (01389) 751234 ❸ 10.30–14.30, 18.30–23.00 Mon–Sat, 11.30–22.00 Sun

## ACCOMMODATION

Accommodation in the region ranges from basic bed and breakfast
to historic coaching inns and luxurious modern spa hotels. A wide
range of places to stay to suit all budgets can be found and booked
online at ⓦ www.visit-lochlomond.com.

**Rowardennan Hotel £** This cosy 3-star hotel's modern facilities
– including two bars and a good restaurant – belie its 310-year
history as a country inn. ❷ Rowardennan village ❶ (01360) 870273
ⓦ www.rowardennanhotel.co.uk

**Black Bull Hotel ££** Very comfortable 19th-century coaching inn
in Killearn in the foothills of the Trossachs with en suite bathrooms,
room service and a stylish, award-winning restaurant. ❷ 2 The Square,
Killearn ❶ (01360) 550215 ⓦ www.blackbullhotel.com

**De Vere Cameron House Hotel ££** The 5-star Cameron House
combines country-house ambience with modern luxuries such
as an upmarket spa and beauty centre and a huge, heated indoor
pool. A marina and yacht club are next door. ❷ Arden, by Balloch
❶ (01389) 755565 ⓦ www.devere.co.uk

**The Lodge on Loch Lomond £££** The most luxurious hotel on the loch
has hosted heads of state and offers a range of sybaritic rooms and
suites along with its own spa and one of the best restaurants in the
area, Colquhoun's. ❷ Luss ❶ (01436) 860201 ⓦ www.loch-lomond.co.uk

# Stirling & Stirlingshire

Scotland's fifth-largest city – after Glasgow, Edinburgh, Aberdeen and Dundee – is also its newest. Stirling was declared a city as recently as 2002, as part of the Queen's Golden Jubilee Celebrations. For all that, Stirling and the surrounding area are rich in history. The city's name means 'place of strife', and it's best known as the site of two rare Scottish victories in the 14th-century Wars of Independence. Stirling Bridge was where William Wallace's spearmen defeated the troops of King Edward I of England (who was nicknamed 'Langshanks' by the Scots). It was also the site of the Battle of Bannockburn, where Robert the Bruce's foot-soldiers gave the very best of Edward II's knights another sound beating and, as it says in Scotland's unofficial national anthem *Flower of Scotland*, 'sent them homeward to think again'.

Arriving in Stirling, it's easy to see why it has such a pivotal role in Scottish history – its forbidding castle, atop a high crag, commanded the most important route between southern and northern Scotland, and without holding Stirling no invader could hope to conquer the country. The castle is Stirling's most prominent landmark, with the narrow streets of the Old Town stretching eastwards from its gateway towards the banks of the Forth.

## GETTING THERE

The easiest way to get to Stirling is by train from Glasgow Queen Street Station (see page 48). For details of this 35-minute journey, check with **First ScotRail** (① 0845 601 5929 ⓦ www.scotrail.co.uk).

Alternatively, buses leave from Buchanan Bus Station (see page 49) in Glasgow city centre, operated by First and Scottish Citylink Coaches (see page 120).

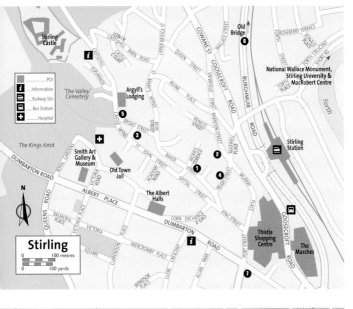

## Stirling

POI ............

Information ![i]

Railway Stn ![train]

Bus Station ![bus]

Hospital ![+]

Stirling Castle

'The Valley' Cemetery

Argyll's Lodging

The Kings Knot

Smith Art Gallery & Museum

Old Town Jail

The Albert Halls

National Wallace Monument, Stirling University & MacRobert Centre

Stirling Station

Thistle Shopping Centre

The Marches

0 ____ 100 metres
0 ____ 100 yards

N

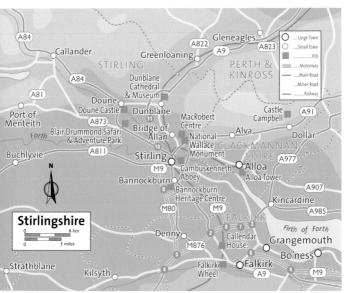

## Stirlingshire

Large Town ◯

Small Town ◯

POI ■

Motorway ===

Main Road ===

Minor Road ---

Railway

Callander

Gleneagles

Greenloaning

STIRLING

PERTH & KINROSS

Doune

Doune Castle

Dunblane Cathedral & Museum

Dunblane

Castle Campbell

Port of Menteith

Blair Drummond Safari & Adventure Park

Bridge of Allan

MacRobert Centre

Alva

Dollar

CLACKMANNANSHIRE

Buchlyvie

Stirling

National Wallace Monument

Alloa

Alloa Tower

Bannockburn

Cambuskenneth Abbey

Bannockburn Heritage Centre

Kincardine

FALKIRK

Denny

Callendar House

Firth of Forth

Grangemouth

Bo'ness

Strathblane

Kilsyth

Falkirk Wheel

Falkirk

Stirling

0 ____ 6 km
0 ____ 3 miles

N

## SIGHTS & ATTRACTIONS

### Alloa Tower

The 14th-century ancestral home of the Erskine Earls of Mar is one of Scotland's largest surviving medieval tower houses. Once host to many of Scotland's monarchs – including Mary Queen of Scots – it has undergone major (award-winning) restoration but has kept its pit dungeon, inside well and original oak beams. The house's fascinating history is comprehensively documented here, and illustrated by a magnificent collection of paintings, furniture and silverware plus rotating exhibitions from the family's private collections. ⓐ Alloa Park, Alloa ① 0844 4932129 Ⓦ www.nts.org.uk 🕓 13.00–17.00 Apr–Oct. Admission charge

### Bannockburn & Bannockburn Heritage Centre

South of Stirling, outside the Bannockburn Heritage Centre, a statue of Robert the Bruce mounted on his charger gazes over the site of his famous 1314 victory over Edward II. Inside there are plans of the battlefield, life-size representations of Bruce, Wallace and other warriors of the day, shields and battle banners. In summer, there are frequent Living History presentations and storytelling sessions, and kids can dress up in period costume and try on armour and chain-mail. ⓐ Glasgow Rd, 4 km (2 miles) south of Stirling off the M80 motorway ① 0844 493 2139 Ⓦ www.nts.org.uk 🕓 10.00–17.30 Mar–Oct. Admission charge

### Blair Drummond Safari & Adventure Park

Wallabies, chimps, elephants and camels are among the exotic beasts that can be enjoyed here. There's also a theme park with water rides and bumper cars among other attractions. ⓐ Between Doune and

Stirling on the A84 ☎ (01786) 841456 🌐 www.blairdrummond.com
🕐 10.00–17.30 Mar–Oct

**Cambuskenneth Abbey**

Founded by the Augustinian order in 1147, the abbey lies in picturesque
ruins just outside Stirling. Though only its tower still stands, this
was once a grand and influential religious foundation, where
Robert the Bruce convened Scotland's first parliament after his
victories over England in 1326. 📍 2 km (1 mile) east of Stirling
town centre ☎ (0131) 668 8800 🌐 www.historic-scotland.gov.uk
🕐 24 hrs Apr–Sept ℹ No access to interior

**Castle Campbell**

This dour stronghold was one of the eastern outposts of the
Campbell clan, whose lands stretched from Argyll on the west
coast as far east as Perthshire. Poised between the Highlands and
Lowlands, the Campbell potentates used their strategic position
to their advantage and became the most powerful of the clan
names, with a canny ability to pick the winning side in Scotland's
centuries of strife. Their aristocratic descendants are still among
the wealthiest and greatest landowners in Scotland. Built in the
15th century, the partly ruined castle is surrounded by terraced
gardens and looks out over the picturesque woodlands of Dollar
Glen. You can get there by car, or by bus from Stirling – in summer,
it's a very pleasant and quite energetic 20-minute walk from the
Dollar Glen bus stop through the wooded glen. 📍 16 km (10 miles)
east of Stirling on the A91 ☎ (01259) 742408 🌐 www.historic-
scotland.gov.uk 🕐 09.30–17.30 Apr–Sept; 09.30–16.30 Oct;
09.30–16.30 Sat–Wed, Nov–Mar. Admission charge

## NATIONAL WALLACE MONUMENT

On the outskirts of Stirling, and just as prominent a landmark as Stirling Castle itself, is the Wallace Monument, standing on a hilltop above the surrounding farmlands. The monument looms above a recent statue of Wallace. Jarringly, his features are those not of a medieval Scottish warlord but of Australian-American film star Mel Gibson, who played Wallace in the movie *Braveheart* in 1995. ❸ Abbey Craig, Hillfoot Rd, Stirling, 3 km (1½ miles) north of the town centre ❶ (01786) 472140 Ⓦ www.nationalwallacemonument.com ⏱ 10.00–17.00 Apr–June, Sept & Oct, 10.00–18.00 July & Aug, 10.30–16.00 Nov–Mar. Admission charge

### Doune Castle

Doune, 13 km (8 miles) northwest of Stirling, was traditionally a meeting place between the wild clanspeople of the Scottish Highlands and the more civilised folk of the Lowlands. Highlanders brought cattle to sell and bought Lowland products such as textiles and firearms including the famous Doune flintlock pistols. Doune is a pretty little village, and the splendid 14th-century Doune Castle with its grand hall was a seat of the Stewart Earls of Moray. ❸ Castle Rd, Doune ❶ (01786) 841742 Ⓦ www.historic-scotland.gov.uk ⏱ 09.30–17.00 Apr–Sept, 09.30–16.30 Oct–Mar. Admission charge

### Dunblane Cathedral & Museum

Dunblane, standing in the glen of the Allan Water 10 km (6 miles) north of Stirling, has one imposing landmark – its gracious cathedral. Founded during the reign of King David I and lavishly restored in 1892,

⬤ *The Victorian Gothic monument to William Wallace*

its vivid stained-glass windows were added in the early 20th century. Dunblane Museum, housed in the vaults of a 17th-century mansion next door, has a collection that highlights the history of the cathedral and the life of its founder, the eponymous St Blane. ⓐ The Cross, Dunblane ⓣ (01786) 825691 ⓦ www.dunblanemuseum.org.uk ⓛ 10.30–16.30 Mon–Sat, May–Sept

### Falkirk, Callendar House, the Falkirk Wheel & Antonine Wall

Falkirk, 19 km (12 miles) south of Stirling, is now almost entirely a residential suburb, poised midway between Glasgow and Edinburgh. That said, it has a handful of attractions spanning 2,000 years of history, from the Roman Empire to the heyday of the Industrial Revolution. **Callendar House** (ⓐ Callendar Park, Falkirk ⓣ (01324) 503770 ⓦ www.falkirk.gov.uk ⓛ 10.00–17.00 Mon–Sat; also open 14.00–17.00 Sun, Apr–Sept) is a stately home that, in its day, hosted Mary Queen of Scots, Oliver Cromwell and Bonnie Prince Charlie among other notables. Its varied exhibits are an interesting introduction to the region's history, especially the Industrial Revolution of the 18th and 19th centuries, when Falkirk was transformed from a small market town into a major powerhouse of the Age of Steam.

The town's biggest attraction is the **Falkirk Wheel** (ⓐ Lime Rd, Tamfourhill, Falkirk ⓣ 0870 050 0208 ⓦ www.thefalkirkwheel.co.uk ⓛ 09.30–18.00 Apr–Oct, 09.30–16.30 Nov–Mar). Completed in 2002, this stunning piece of 21st-century engineering is visually remarkable in its own right and has reconnected two equally remarkable feats of 18th-century engineering – the Forth and Clyde Canal and the Union Canal, one 35 m (115 ft) above the other. The huge boat-lift now hoists boats between the two waterways, which have been reborn as a superb leisure resource for Scotland. It's amazing just to watch the Wheel in action from the Visitor Centre, and you can also board a boat to ride the Wheel and the two canals.

In AD 82 the Roman general Agricola brought his legions into Caledonia and defeated the massed Pictish tribes at the Battle of Mons Graupius – a famous victory. But after this triumph the Romans promptly fell back, and in AD 122 Emperor Hadrian subsequently ordered the building of a coast-to-coast rampart to keep the Picts at bay. His more ambitious successor, Antoninus Pius, pushed north again and built a new defensive line, the **Antonine Wall** (ⓐ Next to the A803 east of Bonnybridge, 19 km (12 miles) south of Stirling ☎ (0131) 668 8800 ⓦ www.historic-scotland.gov.uk), between the Forth and Clyde estuaries. This 60 km (37 mile) fortification was abandoned less than 20 years later, but remnants of it can be seen near Falkirk.

### Falkirk Wheel Boat Trips

Board a modern canal cruiser for a dizzying 35 m (115 ft) ride on the Falkirk Wheel, then cruise through the Union Canal's Roughcastle Tunnel before descending again to the Forth and Clyde Canal. ⓐ Falkirk Wheel, Lime Rd, Tamfourhill, Falkirk ☎ 0870 050 0208 ⓦ www.thefalkirkwheel.co.uk ⏰ 09.30–16.30 Apr–Oct, 10.30–16.30 Nov–Mar. Admission charge

### Stirling Castle

Not for nothing is Stirling Castle known as 'the key to the kingdom'. From its ramparts, 76 m (250 ft) above sea level, there are sweeping views of the lowlands below and the River Forth, though the battlefield of Bannockburn is now covered with suburban homes. The castle's grim exterior belies a more genteel world within, with landscaped gardens and a splendid royal palace. Its Great Hall, which was built during the reign of King James IV and embellished with Renaissance wings built for his successor, James V, is the largest hall

of any Scottish palace or castle. Mary Queen of Scots was crowned in the castle's Royal Chapel in 1543 and her son James was baptised there in 1566. After the Union of the Crowns of Scotland and England in 1603 – when James VI of Scotland also became James I of England – Stirling lost its key role as a royal residence, but the castle remained strategically important in the troubled times of the late 17th and early 18th centuries. The castle houses the regimental museum of the Argyll and Sutherland Highlanders, the oldest of Britain's kilted Highland regiments. History aside, the castle is now also an occasional venue for open-air performances by classical music ensembles and rock bands on summer evenings. The nearby Argyll's

◔ *The forbidding exterior of Stirling Castle*

Lodging, a restored 17th-century townhouse, is also worth a visit.
❷ Castle Wynd ❶ (01786) 450000 ❸ www.stirlingcastle.gov.uk
❹ 09.30–18.00 Apr–Sept; 09.30–17.00 Oct–Mar

### Stirling Ghost Walk

A spooky, guided walk through the haunted, cobbled wynds
(alleyways) of the Old Town, below the castle. Bookings and
information from the Argyll, Loch Lomond & the Forth Valley
Tourist Board (see page 152).

### Stirling Old Bridge

This stands roughly where Wallace's Scottish freedom fighters won
their first victory against Edward I. Built in the late 15th century –
almost two centuries after that fight – it was blown up in 1745
to delay the advance of Bonnie Prince Charlie's Highlanders,
and repaired four years later. ❷ On the River Forth off the M9
at Stirling ❶ (0131) 668 8800 ❸ www.historic-scotland.gov.uk

### Stirling Old Town Jail

Across Castle Wynd from Argyll's Lodging is a Victorian prison that
has been turned into a slightly kitsch visitor attraction, with actors
playing out the roles of convicts, warders and hangmen. ❷ 31 St Johns St,
Stirling ❶ (01786) 450050 ❸ www.oldtownjail.com ❹ 10.00–17.00
June–Oct. Admission charge

## CULTURE

### MacRobert Centre

If you are of an artistic persuasion this is the place for you, with
galleries, drama and cinema on offer. ❷ Stirling University Campus

◔ *Stirling Old Bridge is one of Scotland's most historic locations*

☎ (01786) 466666 ⓦ www.macrobert.stir.ac.uk ⏰ Hours vary, so phone to check

### Smith Art Gallery & Museum

This gallery is well worth a visit for its eclectic collection of objects from around the world – most of them donated by local people who had lived and worked abroad as engineers, soldiers, doctors and administrators during the heyday of the British Empire. The museum was a bequest to the city by painter and collector Thomas Stuart Smith (1815–69) and its art gallery displays a plethora of landscapes, battlefield scenes and portraits of local bigwigs. The high point is the portrait of the Young Pretender, Charles Edward Stuart –

better known as Bonnie Prince Charlie. ❸ Dumbarton Rd
❶ (01786) 471917 🅦 www.smithartgallery.demon.co.uk
🄻 10.30–17.00 Tues–Sat, 14.00–17.00 Sun

## TAKING A BREAK

**Nicky Tams £ ❶** A cosy wee pub a short walk from Stirling Castle.
The reputedly haunted bar and former bank has an old look, but
attracts punters of all ages and lots of students. ❸ 29 Baker St,
Stirling ❶ (01786) 472194 🅦 www.nickytamsbar.co.uk 🄻 11.30–23.00
Mon–Fri, 11.30–00.00 Sat, 11.30–22.30 Sun

**Smiling Jack's £ ❷** Extremely cheap – considering the size of the
portions – and very cheerful, this Tex-Mex joint is for those with a
hearty appetite to satisfy. ❸ 17 Barnton St, Stirling ❶ (01786) 462809
🄻 11.30–23.30 Mon–Sat

**The Tolbooth £ ❸** A bright, modern café-bar within a lively arts
centre, handy for the castle and Old Town sights. ❸ Jail Wynd,
Stirling ❶ (01786) 274000 🄻 12.00–23.30 Mon–Sat, 12.00–23.00 Sun

**La Ciociara ££ ❹** Popular Italian café and gelateria serving up snacks
and ice cream throughout the day downstairs and meals in the
restaurant above. Great for people-watching. ❸ 41 Friars St, Stirling
❶ (01786) 451552 🄻 11.00–22.00 Sun–Thur, 11.00–23.00 Fri & Sat

**Hermann's ££ ❺** Simply the best restaurant in Stirling, serving simple,
fresh Scottish seafood, game and local produce, elegantly prepared.
❸ Mar Place House, Stirling ❶ (01786) 450632 🅦 www.hermanns.co.uk
🄻 11.00–23.00 Mon–Sat

**Jekyll's ££ ⑥** Stylish hotel restaurant – the only place in town that can compete with Hermann's, and surprisingly good value despite its upmarket pretensions. ⓐ Queen's Hotel, 24 Henderson St, Stirling ① (01786) 833268 ⓛ 11.00–23.00 Mon–Sat, 11.30–23.00 Sun

**Zingermans ££ ⑦** Modern Scottish restaurant serving breakfasts until 11.30am, high tea in the afternoon, lunchtime sandwiches and risotto through to rib-eyes and langoustines for dinner. Dom Pérignon by the glass, too. Delicious. ⓐ 52 Port St, Stirling ① (01786) 463222 ⓦ www.zingermans.co.uk ⓛ 07.00–22.00

## ACCOMMODATION

**Glenardoch House £** A charming B&B set in an 18th-century house on the banks of the river and in the shadow of Doune Castle, with extensive gardens. ⓐ Castle Rd, Doune ① 0845 225 5121 ⓦ www.glenardochhouse.com

**Park Lodge Country House Hotel £** Excellent value at this Georgian hotel with views of the castle. ⓐ 32 Park Terrace, Stirling ① (01786) 474862 ⓦ www.parklodge.net

**Stirling Highland Hotel ££** A former Victorian school in the centre of Stirling now makes for a wonderfully elegant place to stay in the city. There's also a leisure club on site. ⓐ Spittal St, Stirling ① 0870 116 0602 ⓦ www.barcelo-hotels.co.uk

⊙ *Kelvingrove Park has something for everyone*

# PRACTICAL
information

# Directory

## GETTING THERE
### By air
Glasgow International Airport (see page 48) is serviced by several daily scheduled flights from major British and European cities, and there are some 40 flights a day from London to Glasgow. Flight time from London is one hour. International flights cover Asian, North African and US destinations, as well as Europe. If you're looking for the cheapest option, the low-cost no-frills airline **Ryanair** (W www.ryanair.com) operates flights from various smaller airports in the UK and Europe to Glasgow.

Many people are aware that air travel emits $CO_2$, which contributes to climate change. You may be interested in the possibility of lessening the environmental impact of your flight through the charity **Climate Care** (W www.climatecare.org), which offsets your $CO_2$ by funding environmental projects around the world.

### By rail
The **East Coast** (T 084578 225111 W www.eastcoast.co.uk) rail route from London Euston or King's Cross to Glasgow Central Station (see page 48) takes between four and a half and five and a half hours on the direct route, although some services require a change of trains. The monthly *Thomas Cook European Rail Timetable* (T +44 1733 416 477 W www.thomascookpublishing.com) has up-to-date train timetables for the UK and Europe.

### By road
National Express coaches (see page 49) make the journey between London and Glasgow seven times a day, with an average journey time

of between eight and a half and ten hours, depending on traffic and time of day. **Megabus** (t 0900 160 0900 w www.megabus.com) is a budget coach service that also links Glasgow with London and runs three services a day, one of which operates overnight.

If you want to drive yourself, Glasgow is easily reached by the M6/M74 motorway from the west of Britain and by the M8 from Edinburgh. Both the **AA** (w www.theaa.com) and the **RAC** (w www.rac.co.uk) offer route-planning services on their websites to help plan your journey.

*Glasgow's Central Station*

## ENTRY FORMALITIES

Entry and visa requirements for Scotland are the same as for the rest of the UK. EU, US, Canadian, Australian and New Zealand citizens must have a valid passport, but do not need a visa. Visitors from other countries may need a visa to enter the UK and should contact their consulate or embassy before departure. More information on visas is available at Ⓦ www.ukvisas.gov.uk.

## MONEY

The national currency is the British pound (GBP), which is divided into 100 pence. ATM machines are plentiful in the city centre and accept most major credit and debit cards including Visa and MasterCard. Most restaurants, hotels and department stores accept Visa, MasterCard and American Express. Many shops, especially in areas frequented by tourists, also accept card payments.

One aspect that often confuses visitors to Scotland is that Scottish banknotes come in three different designs, representing the Bank of Scotland, the Royal Bank of Scotland and the Clydesdale Bank. English banknotes are, however, entirely legal tender in Scotland. It might be advisable to change Scottish banknotes back into English banknotes at the end of your stay. Even in England, where they are also legal tender, many smaller shopkeepers can be confused by them and refuse to take them, and they are extremely difficult to exchange abroad.

## HEALTH, SAFETY & CRIME

Visitors to Scotland are unlikely to encounter any food or drink issues – tap water is safe to drink, although bottled water is also available everywhere.

Medical facilities are run by the National Health Service (NHS), which entitles British and EU citizens to free medical care. Visitors from outside these areas should make sure they have adequate health insurance to avoid having to pay for any medical care should they fall ill. If you take prescription drugs, make sure you bring an adequate supply as well as a letter from your doctor or a personal health record card. Most minor ailments can be diagnosed and treated at pharmacies throughout the city and, unlike many other countries, mild pain relief, such as aspirin, can often be bought at small grocery shops and in supermarkets, as well as at pharmacies.

Glasgow is generally a safe city, particularly in the tourist areas, but common sense applies as it does everywhere in terms of personal possessions. In crowded areas and in pubs keep an eye on bags and wallets. Large crowds of Celtic and Rangers football supporters are probably best avoided on match days. Any crime should be reported to the police straightaway. Police can be seen regularly on the streets, dressed in black-and-white uniform and, often, fluorescent yellow jackets. They are friendly and efficient, and can be approached for anything from asking directions to reporting crime.

For advice on what to do in an emergency, see page 154.

## OPENING HOURS

Most shops in Glasgow open from 09.00 to 17.30 Monday to Saturday and 10.00 to 16.00 Sunday. Some shopping centres and department stores open later on Thursdays. The majority of the city's key attractions open from 10.00 to 17.00 daily. Some open later during the summer months. Banks generally open from 09.00 to 17.00 Monday to Saturday, although some smaller branches may close at the weekend.

## TOILETS

Toilet facilities can be found in museums, department stores and shopping centres, and are generally clean and of a high standard.

In pubs you would normally be expected to buy a drink before using the facilities, although many landlords and bar staff will kindly overlook this.

## CHILDREN

Glasgow is a child-friendly city and, with the smoking ban in place, even most pubs will be happy to have children on their premises, although it's always best to check first. All but the top restaurants will welcome children, and many offer children's menus. Baby food, nappies and other kiddie paraphernalia can be bought in supermarkets, in high-street chain pharmacies and at grocery stores.

Many attractions are specifically geared towards children, including the Glasgow Science Centre (see page 92), the Scotland Street School Museum (see page 101), and the **Scottish Mask and Puppet Centre** (ⓐ 8–10 Balcarres Avenue ① (0141) 339 6185), where they can learn to make puppets and masks. Slightly older children will also get a lot out of the natural history section of the Kelvingrove Art Gallery & Museum (see page 82). Just outside Glasgow in Tollcross Park there's a **Children's Zoo** (① (0141) 552 1142).

## COMMUNICATIONS
### Internet

Glasgow is extensively wired (and wireless). Internet cafés are dotted all over the city and you're never likely to be more than a few minutes away from web and email access.

**Sip & Surf** ⓐ 521 Great Western Rd, Glasgow ① (0141) 339 4449 ⓛ 08.00–22.00 Mon–Fri, 09.00–22.00 Sat & Sun

**Yeeha Internet** ⓐ 48 West George St, Glasgow ① (0141) 332 6543 ⓛ 07.00–21.00

**TELEPHONING GLASGOW**
To phone Glasgow from outside the UK, dial your country's international calling code (usually 00), followed by 44 for the UK, followed by 141 for Glasgow, followed by the seven-digit number. To call Glasgow from another city in the UK, simply dial 0141 and the seven-digit number.

**TELEPHONING ABROAD**
To phone abroad from anywhere in Scotland, dial 00 followed by the country code and the local number. Country codes are listed in the phone directory and include: Australia 61; Canada 1; France 33; Germany 49; Ireland 353; New Zealand 64; USA 1.

### Phone
Public payphones accept coins, phone cards or credit cards. Phone cards are available from post offices and newsagents in different values from £2.00 to £20.00. Some payphones also offer the option of texting messages. The minimum rate for a cash call is around 30 pence; the minimum rate for a credit card call is around 95 pence. As in the rest of the world, making phone calls from hotel rooms is exorbitantly expensive, and so best avoided if possible.

### Post
The British postal service is generally very reliable, with first-class mail arriving at UK destinations usually within one day, and in Europe within two or three days (depending on the service at the country of destination). The main post office in the city centre is in St Vincent Street, but there are other central branches in Merchant

City and on Bothwell Street and Hope Street. Post offices are usually open all day (09.00 to 17.30 Monday to Friday and 09.00 to 12.00 Saturday), although smaller branches often close for lunch. Stamps can be bought at post offices, as well as at larger newsagents. Post boxes on the street are the round, red pillar boxes, some of which have separate slots for national and international mail. For enquiries contact the **Post Office Customer Helpline** (☎ 0845 722 3344 ⓦ www.postoffice.co.uk).

## ELECTRICITY

The standard electrical voltage in Britain is 240 volts with square three-pinned plugs. Foreign appliances will require an adaptor plug, available at airports and from most travel and electrical shops.

## TRAVELLERS WITH DISABILITIES

In general, Glasgow takes the issue of disability very seriously indeed. However, many of Glasgow's older buildings, including pubs, may be difficult to access for wheelchair users – even if you are able to enter the establishment, you may not be able to use the toilet facilities. Newer establishments, however, including museums, restaurants and bars, build disabled access into their design by law.

Capability Scotland provides advice and information about disability issues, while the Glasgow Access Panel has an excellent website detailing disabled access to all manner of places in the city, including churches, restaurants and shops. Tourism for All is a national organisation that offers advice about holidays around Britain and transport issues for those with disabilities. RADAR provides a similar service, as well as offering advice to visitors from other countries. **Capability Scotland** ⓐ 11 Ellersly Rd, Edinburgh EH12 6HY

ⓣ (0131) 337 9876 Ⓦ www.capability-scotland.org.uk

**Glasgow Access Panel** Ⓐ Unit 17, Chapel St Estate, Maryhill, Glasgow
G20 9BQ ⓣ (0141) 946 8488 Ⓦ www.glasgowaccesspanel.org.uk

**RADAR** Ⓐ 12 City Forum, 250 City Rd, London EC1V 8AF
ⓣ (0207) 250 3222 Ⓦ www.radar.org.uk

**Tourism for All** Ⓐ Shap Rd Industrial Estate, Shap Rd, Kendal,
Cumbria LA9 6NZ ⓣ 0845 124 9971 Ⓦ www.tourismforall.org.uk

◆ *A waterbus ride on the River Clyde offers great views of the city*

## TOURIST INFORMATION

The city's main tourist office is centrally located at George Square near the bus station and stocks a range of leaflets, literature, guides and maps of the city and the surrounding area, as well as a small selection of souvenirs. Staff are knowledgeable and helpful, and can offer advice on attractions, eating out, current events, accommodation and theatre tickets (including handling bookings), day trips and much more. There's also a very good information centre at Glasgow International Airport, near the arrivals and departures area. This and other tourist information facilities can be found at:

**Glasgow International Airport** ☏ 0844 481 5555

**Hamilton Tourist Information Centre** ⓐ RoadChef Services, M74 (northbound), Hamilton ☏ (01698) 285590

**Lanark Tourist Information Centre** ⓐ Horsemarket, Ladyacre Rd, Lanark ☏ (01555) 661661

**Paisley Tourist Information Centre** ⓐ 9a Gilmour St, Paisley ☏ (0141) 889 0711

The official tourist office website for Scotland is ⓦ www.visitscotland.com, while you can find detailed information on Scotland's historical attractions by visiting ⓦ www.historic-scotland.gov.uk. A useful (unofficial) information website is ⓦ www.glasgowguide.co.uk.

If you are venturing out towards Loch Lomond, the Trossachs or Stirlingshire, check the **Argyll, Loch Lomond & the Forth Valley website** at ⓦ www.visitscottishheartlands.com. The most useful tourist information centres in these areas are:

**Balloch** ⓐ Balloch Rd, Balloch ☏ 08707 200 607

**Callandar** ⓐ Ancaster Square, Callander ☏ 08707 200 628

**Falkirk Wheel** ⓐ Lime Rd, Tamfourhill, Falkirk ☏ 08707 200 614

**Stirling** ⓐ 41 Dumbarton Rd, Stirling ☏ 08707 200 620

## BACKGROUND READING

*Charles Rennie Mackintosh* by John McKean. A history of the man and his work, illustrated with examples.

*Dick Donovan: The Glasgow Detective* by James Emmerson Preston Muddock. A reprint of the popular Victorian detective series.

*Glasgow Tales* by Rachel Hazelwood (ed.). A collection of short stories set in the modern city.

*How Late it Was, How Late* by James Kelman. The 1994 Booker Prize winner is a stream of consciousness tale about alcoholism and police brutality in rain-soaked Glasgow.

*Lanark* by Alasdair Gray. A blend of surrealism and realism set in the outskirts of Glasgow.

*Night Song of the Last Tram: A Glasgow Childhood* by Robert Douglas. Autobiographical account of growing up in a Glasgow tenement.

*Once Upon a Time in Glasgow* by John Watson. A full history of the city.

*Para Handy* by Neil Munro. A collection of Munro's classic tales of Clyde mariner Para Handy and his crew as they sail between Glasgow and the Highlands.

*Rob Roy* by Sir Walter Scott. The classic, heavily romanticised tale of Rob Roy McGregor.

*The Trick is to Keep Breathing* by Janice Galloway. Acclaimed tale of living on a Glasgow housing scheme.

*Weegies v Edinbuggers* by Ian Black. A humorous look at the rivalry between the two Scottish cities.

# Emergencies

The following are free nationwide emergency numbers:

**Police, fire & ambulance** ℹ 999

**European emergency number** ℹ 112 (This is the standard SOS number in all EU countries. The operator will connect you to the service you need.)

ℹ When you dial the UK emergency services number 999:

- ask for the service you require
- give details of where you are, what the emergency is and the number of the phone you are using.

🔺 *A blue police box opposite the Cathedral*

## MEDICAL SERVICES
### Dental
For dental problems visit the **Glasgow Dental Hospital**
🏢 378 Sauchiehall St ☎ (0141) 211 9600 🕐 09.00–17.00 Mon–Fri

### Hospitals
There are four main hospitals in Glasgow with accident and
emergency departments:
**Glasgow Royal Infirmary** 🏢 Castle St ☎ (0141) 211 4000
**Glasgow Western Infirmary** 🏢 Dumbarton Rd ☎ (0141) 211 2000
**Southern General Hospital** 🏢 1345 Govan Rd ☎ (0141) 201 1100
**Stobhill Hospital** 🏢 133 Balornock Rd ☎ (0141) 201 3000

## POLICE
The police headquarters for central Glasgow are at 🏢 173 Pitt St
☎ (0141) 532 2000. The most central police station in Glasgow, however,
is at 🏢 945 Argyle St ☎ (0141) 532 3200. If you lose any belongings through
negligence rather than theft, call the police headquarters number.

## EMBASSIES & CONSULATES
There are no embassies or consulates for the following countries in
Glasgow itself. The nearest branches are in Edinburgh, as follows:
**Australia** 🏢 2 Festival Square ☎ (0131) 228 4771 🌐 www.uk.embassy.gov.au
**Canada** 🏢 50 Lothian Rd, Festival Square ☎ (0131) 473 6320
🌐 www.canadainternational.gc.ca
**New Zealand** 🏢 5 Rutland Square ☎ (0131) 222 8109
🌐 www.nzembassy.com
**Republic of Ireland** 🏢 16 Randolph Crescent ☎ (0131) 226 7711
🌐 www.irishconsulatescotland.co.uk
**USA** 🏢 3 Regent Terrace ☎ (0131) 556 8315 🌐 www.usembassy.org.uk

## A

accommodation 34–9
  Loch Lomond 129
  Stirling 142
air travel 48, 144
Alloa Tower 132
Amazonia 106–8
Antonine Wall 137
arts see culture
Auchentoshan
  Distillery 120, 126

## B

background reading 153
bagpipes 69
Balloch 120
Balloch Castle
  Country Park 121
Bannockburn 132
Barras, The 23, 70
bars & pubs see nightlife
Bellahouston Park 90
Ben Lomond 121
Blair Drummond
  Safari Park 132–3
boat trips 94, 97, 111,
  120, 137
Botanic Gardens 78–80
Bothwell Castle 108
Burrell Collection 97–8
bus travel 49, 54–6, 106,
  120, 130, 144–5

## C

cafés
  city centre 72–4
  Loch Lomond 127–9
  Southside 102
  Stirling 141–2
  West End 86
Calderglen Country
  Park 108
Callendar House 136
Cambuskenneth
  Abbey 133

camping 39
car hire 58
Castle Campbell 133
Celtic FC Visitor Centre 32,
  90–1
Celtic Park 32
Centre for Contemporary
  Arts 65–6
Chatelherault
  Country Park 108–10
children 148
cinema 28
City Chambers 60
Clyde Valley 106–17
Clydebuilt Scottish
  Maritime Museum 98
Collins Gallery 66
comedy 12–13, 28–30
Craignethan Castle 110–11
crime 52, 147
Crookston Castle 92
culture 18–20

## D

disabled travellers 150–1
Dollan Aqua Centre 111
Doune Castle 134
driving 52, 56–8, 120, 145
Dumbarton 121
Dumbarton Rock
  & Castle 121–2
Dunblane Cathedral
  & Museum 134–6

## E

electricity 150
embassies &
  consulates 155
emergencies 154–5
entertainment
  see nightlife
events 8–11, 12–13

## F

Falkirk &
  Falkirk Wheel 136–7

Falls of Clyde 111
festivals 8–11, 12–13
food & drink 24–7
football 32, 90–2,
  93–4, 100
Forth & Clyde
  Canal Cruises 111
Fossil Grove 80

## G

Gallery of Modern Art 66
Glasgow Cathedral 60–2
Glasgow Cookery
  School 46
Glasgow Green 64
Glasgow Police
  Museum 66
Glasgow School
  of Art 68–9
Glasgow Science Centre 92
Glengoyne Distillery 122–3
go-karting 46

## H

haggis 27
Hampden Park 31
health 146–7, 155
Hidden Gardens 44
history 14–15
hotels
  see accommodation
House for an Art Lover
  98–100
Hunter House
  Museum 113
Hunterian Art Gallery &
  Museum 82

## I

Ibrox Stadium 32
Inchmurrin 123–4
internet 148

## J

James Hamilton
  Heritage Park 111–13

**K**

Kelvingrove Art Gallery
    & Museum 82–3

**L**

lifestyle 16–17
listings 30
Loch Lomond 118–29
Loch Lomond islands 123–5
lost property 155
Luss 118–20

**M**

Mackintosh, CR 20, 62,
    68–9, 74, 82, 98–100,
    101, 153
Mackintosh House 82
MacRobert Centre 139–40
Magners Glasgow
    Comedy Festival 12–13
Mansfield Park 27
markets 23, 27
Martyrs' School 62
Merchant City 62–4
Mitchell Library 80
money 146
Motherwell Heritage
    Centre 113–14
Museum of
    Transport 83–4
music 18–20, 28–31, 69

**N**

National Museum
    of Rural Life 114
National Piping Centre 69
National Theatre
    of Scotland 18
National Wallace
    Monument 134
Necropolis 60–2
New Lanark World
    Heritage Village 114–16
nightlife 28–31
    city centre 77
    Southside 104

**O**

opening hours 147

**P**

Paisley Abbey 113
Paisley Museum 116
passports & visas 146
People's Palace 64
phone 149
police 154–5
Pollok House & Park 92–3
post 149–50
Provand's Lordship 64–5
public holidays 11
public transport 48–9,
    52–6, 106, 120, 130, 144–5

**R**

rail travel 48, 106, 130, 144
Rangers Football
    Club 93–4
restaurants 24–7
    city centre 74–7
    Clyde Valley 117
    Loch Lomond 127–9
    Southside 103–4
    Stirling 141–2
    West End 86–9
Royal Highland
    Fusiliers Museum 69
Ruchill Church Hall 82

**S**

safety 52, 147
St Mungo Museum 69–70
sailing 126–7
Scotland Street
    School Museum 101
Scottish Exhibition &
    Conference Centre 94
Scottish Football
    Museum 100
Scottish Mask &
    Puppet Centre 148
Scottish Wildlife Trust 111

Seaforce boat tours 94
seasons 8
shopping 22–3
    city centre 70–2
    Loch Lomond 126–7
    Southside 101–2
    West End 84–5
Smith Art Gallery
    & Museum 140–1
smoking 16–17, 26
sport 32–3, 126–7
Stirling &
    Stirlingshire 130–42
Stirling Castle 137–9
Stirling Ghost Walk 139
Stirling Old Bridge 139
Stirling Old Town Jail 139
Strathclyde
    Country Park 110
subway 56
Summerlee Heritage
    Centre 117
symbols &
    abbreviations 4

**T**

Tall Ship, The 94–7
taxis 56
Tenement House 65
theatre 18
time difference 48
tipping 24
toilets 147–8
tourist information 152
Trades Hall 65
Trossachs National
    Park 118–29

**W**

walking 127
Wallace Monument 134
Waverley, The 97
weather 8, 46–7
whisky 27, 120

Editorial/project management: Lisa Plumridge
Copy editor: Monica Guy
Layout/DTP: Alison Rayner

The publishers would like to thank the following individuals and organisations for supplying their copyright photographs for this book: Pamela Adam, page 89; Martin Alvarez Espinar, page 9; BBC Scottish Symphony Orchestra, page 19; Mike Beltzner, page 154; Phyllis Buchanan, page 10; Renzo Ferrante, page 54; gingiber, pages 124–5; Glasgow City Marketing Bureau, pages 17, 21, 23, 31, 99, 112 & 151; Katherine, page 47; The Rezidor Hotel Group, page 36; The Stand, page 13; Ross Williamson/iStockphoto.com, page 29; Robin Gauldie, all others.

**Send your thoughts to**
# books@thomascook.com

- Found a great bar, club, shop or must-see sight that we don't feature?
- Like to tip us off about any information that needs a little updating?
- Want to tell us what you love about this handy little guidebook and more importantly how we can make it even handier?

Then here's your chance to tell all! Send us ideas, discoveries and recommendations today and then look out for your valuable input in the next edition of this title.

Email the above address (stating the title) or write to:
pocket guides Series Editor, Thomas Cook Publishing, PO Box 227, Coningsby Road, Peterborough PE3 8SB, UK.

## WHAT'S IN YOUR GUIDEBOOK?

**Independent authors** Impartial up-to-date information from our travel experts who meticulously source local knowledge.

**Experience** Thomas Cook's 165 years in the travel industry and guidebook publishing enriches every word with expertise you can trust.

**Travel know-how** Thomas Cook has thousands of staff working around the globe, all living and breathing travel.

**Editors** Travel-publishing professionals, pulling everything together to craft a perfect blend of words, pictures, maps and design.

**You, the traveller** We deliver a practical, no-nonsense approach to information, geared to how you really use it.

## ABOUT THE AUTHOR

Zoë Ross is an editor and travel writer who has written several guide books for Thomas Cook, the AA and many other publishers, as well as contributing articles to national newspapers and in-flight magazines. London-born, she now lives in Edinburgh and visits Glasgow regularly.

Thomas Cook **pocket** guides

# PARIS

Your travelling companion since 1873

Thomas Cook

…shed
…nds,
…avel.

…s our
…crets
…orld,
…th of
…ravi

…yo
…t trip
…tage.